7,500 CRAPS ROLLS

7,500 CRAPS ROLLS

THOMAS MIDGLEY

GBC PRESS
P. O. Box 98115
Las Vegas, NV 89193
www.gamblersbookclub.com

GBC Press books are published by Gambler's Books Club in Las Vegas, Nevada. Since 1964, the legendary GBC has been the reigning authority on gambling publications and the only dedicated gambling bookstore anywhere.

Library of Congress Catalog Number: 2011925832
ISBN 10: 1-58042-283-7   ISBN 13: 978-1-58042-283-3
GBC Press is an imprint of Cardoza Publishing

GBC PRESS
c/o Cardoza Publishing
P.O. Box 98115, Las Vegas, NV 89193
Toll-Free Phone (800)522-1777
email: info@gamblersbookclub.com
www.gamblersbookclub.com

About the Author

Thomas Midgley, an engineer who graduated from Cornell University, rolled his first natural in a home craps game when he was only five years old, beating his father out of a few dollars. He later used his mathematical training and love for the game to analyze how dice perform. He found out that the dice operate in cycles—and discovered why most systems players lose.

Midgley did not use computer simulations to generate his statistics. He got his data in real games with live players, standing alongside other players at noisy crap tables. He painstakingly and accurately recorded 7,500 rolls of the dice while shooting craps at five landmark casinos in Las Vegas. Combining deep analysis of the data with mathematical investigations of crap odds, probabilities, and return ratios, Midgley formulated the powerful ideas in this book.

T TABLE OF CONTENTS

1

INTRODUCTION

By GBC Editors

If you're a serious craps player who wants to beat the casinos and take their money, this is the book for you! It is a study of the actual results that can occur during live casino play, as well as the theoretical results you should expect when you're using various craps betting systems—and how the two can differ.

Thomas Midgley gives you the live casino results of 7,500 dice hands he painstakingly and accurately recorded at five landmark casinos in Las Vegas. You'll see the numbers thrown on the coming out roll and on each subsequent roll in every hand in the order in which the dice produced the numbers. You'll also find out how many rolls each hand lasted and whether each pass bet decision won or lost money for bettors. The value of these results is incalculable for serious craps players looking to get the extra edge.

This is also a great book for developing or testing your own winning systems. Every right-hand page gives you worksheets to record the results of your craps play so that you can see, in black and white, what works and what doesn't. Then you can add your own bottom line—turning a profit at the tables.

This book is about winning, making money at the dice tables. Using the results of Midgley's 7,500 rolls of the dice and deep game analysis, you'll learn how to evaluate your favorite system, test it against reality, and increase your chances of making a profit at craps!

2 ODDS AND PROBABILITIES

There are three mathematical concepts that are vital to your understanding of the game of craps. These three concepts—probability, odds, and return—are the reasons why some bets that you can make at the crap table are far better than other bets. Basically, it's a money matter—you can make more money or lose less money on your bets, depending on their probability, odds and return.

This chapter will show you the odds and probabilities that certain combinations of two die numbers will appear when a pair of dice is thrown across a crap table. I gathered the statistical information on which my analysis is based from playing craps for forty hours at five Las Vegas casinos: the Frontier, the Hilton, Caesars, the Sands and the Golden Nugget. During my forty hours of keeping records, the other shooters and I rolled the bones 7,654 times.

Each time we rolled the dice, I kept meticulous records of the number thrown on the coming out roll and the numbers of each subsequent roll involved in completing each pass bet decision. From these records, I compiled a wealth of statistical data regarding how the dice perform in relation in their theoretical odds and probabilities.

The focus of this research is to show how dice odds and return ratios are calculated in their probability forms. When we express something in terms of its odds, we are stating the number of times an event is likely to happen compared to the number of times the event is likely not to happen.. For example, out of the 36 possible combinations on a pair of dice, one of them is 2 (1 + 1) making the odds against a single roll of 2 on the dice 35 to 1. When we express something in terms of its probabilities, we are stating the ratio of the number of times that an event is likely to happen compared to the whole number of ways of which this particular event is a part. For example, the probability for having two dice add to 2 is 1 out of 36 rolls.

The mathematics of probability in any game of chance is basic to a thorough understanding of the game. It is from the computation of an event's probability that we derive its odds and return ratios. Once you understand the basic math of dice probabilities, you will make far superior betting decisions than the uneducated weekend warriors who keep the casinos in business by taking unnecessary risks on improbable outcomes at the crap table.

Let us begin with a brief review of several odds concepts developed in my first book on dice, *Craps: A Smart Shooter's Guide*.

WHAT ARE THE ODDS?

If a person takes a penny and flips it into the air 100 or so times, letting it fall to the ground each time, regardless of how many times he starts with a head or a tail in the upper position he will have a final result close to 50 heads and 50 tails. These are the correct 50/50 odds for a flat coin that has two differently marked sides. Likewise, if a single die is rolled a large number of times, the final result should show the same number of 1's, 2's, 3's, 4's, 5's, and 6's. This is also true whether two dice are rolled together or six dice are rolled together.

The basic odds for craps are 1,004 to 976 against making a pass, and 976 to 949 against winning with a don't pass bet.

Both of these give return ratios of 98.59% which translates into saying that when you bet either pass or don't pass, you will face the probability of losing $1.41 for each $100 that you wager. As far as casino games go, and the game of craps in particular, these are very attractive return ratios.

During the 40 hours that data was recorded, the dice were thrown 7,654 times, making 15,308 rolls of an individual die. The following tabulation shows the number of times that each die number appeared.

NUMBER OF TIMES EACH DIE NUMBER APPEARED 15,308 Rolls of Individual Dice							
CASINO	1	2	3	4	5	6	TOTAL DIE ROLLS
Frontier	326	402	366	345	351	368	2,158
Hilton	312	316	296	323	294	319	1,860
Caesars	498	524	559	540	493	482	3,096
Sands	485	519	494	491	470	463	2,922
Nugget	877	886	891	891	854	873	5,272
40-Hour Totals	2,498	2,647	2,606	2,590	2,462	2,505	15,308
Probability	2,551	2,551	2,551	2,551	2,551	2,551	

In presenting this data, the theoretical dice probabilities for each casino were not shown, only the theoretical probabilities for the total 40 hours. This same procedure will be followed for all the tabulations in this book. The theoretical probabilities for each casino can be calculated easily should you wish to do so. However, in craps, your overall performance will be determined by how well you perform as a total at all the crap tables in all the casinos in which you gamble, not just in one or two among them. This is the way that most players shoot craps—a little time at one table, followed by short times at other tables.

DICE COMBINATIONS

There are 21 number combinations produced by the two dice and there are 36 dice combinations produced by the two dice. Let's now tabulate the quantities of dice combinations produced by the dice with all their rolls at the five casinos and compare these with their theoretical probabilities.

DICE COMBINATIONS								
DICE ROLL		Frontier	Hilton	Caesars	Sands	Nugget	40-hr total	Probability
2	(1-1)	31	34	43	35	67	210	213
3	(1-2)	60	53	85	78	157	433	425
4	(2-2)	36	33	48	39	69	225	213
	(1-3)	45	46	99	82	159	431	425
5	(1-4)	47	58	70	87	141	403	425
	(2-3)	71	51	85	99	149	455	425
6	(3-3)	31	25	35	38	73	202	213
	(1-5)	53	57	69	78	142	399	425
	(2-4)	75	49	97	91	152	464	425
7	(1-6)	59	30	89	90	144	412	425
	(2-5)	55	45	85	90	146	421	425
	(3-4)	52	52	110	77	141	432	425
8	(4-4)	24	23	49	48	70	214	213
	(2-6)	69	52	76	83	144	424	425
	(3-5)	75	49	94	74	137	429	425
9	(3-6)	61	48	101	86	159	455	425
	(4-5)	56	51	81	69	155	412	425
10	(5-5)	33	15	44	44	65	201	213
	(4-6)	67	67	84	71	162	457	425
11	(5-6)	46	62	76	71	144	399	425
12	(6-6)	33	30	28	31	60	182	213

In the basic game of craps, we are not concerned with the composition of the numbers. We are concerned only with the sum of the numbers on the two dice. Consequently, we can take the foregoing outline of the various dice combinations, which total 36, and consolidate them further.

DICE PROBABILITIES AND EXPECTATIONS

Take a look at the following probability chart.

PROBABILITY	
One way to make a 2	1/36
Two ways to make a 3	2/36
Three ways to make a 4	3/36
Four ways to make a 5	4/36
Five ways to make a 6	5/36
Six ways to make a 7	6/36
Five ways to make an 8	5/36
Four ways to make a 9	4/36
Three ways to make a 10	3/36
Two ways to make an 11	2/36
One way to make a 12	1/36

This chart shows us that each complementary pair of numbers has the same probability: 2 and 12 (1/36), 3 and 11 (2/36), 4 and 10 (3/36), 5 and 9 (4/36), 6 and 8 (5/36), and 7 and 7 (6/36).

Now take a look at the next chart, which shows how the dice performances at all five casinos adhered to their probabilities.

SUM OF BOTH DICE											
	2	3	4	5	6	7	8	9	10	11	12	TOTALS
Frontier	31	60	81	118	159	166	168	117	100	46	33	1,079
Hilton	34	53	79	109	131	127	124	99	82	62	30	930
Caesars	43	85	147	155	201	284	219	182	128	76	28	1,548
Sands	35	78	121	186	207	257	205	155	115	71	31	1,461
Nugget	67	157	228	290	367	431	351	314	227	144	60	2,636
40-hr total	210	433	656	858	1065	1265	1067	867	652	399	182	7,654
Prob-ability	213	425	638	850	1063	1276	1063	850	638	425	213	

CONCLUSIONS

In this chapter we have shown that in producing numbers, dice perform close to what theory dictates they should. No consistent performance of the number on any one die, nor did the performance of any of the numbers produced by both dice, show any consistent non-probability performance at any casino to a degree that could have led to the development of any winning gambling scheme. The dice performed as they should.

It is essential that we accept this fact when attempting to establish a winning course of betting.

3 ROLLS RESULTS

We reviewed the odds for the game of craps in the previous chapter to form a reference point for some of the points made in this chapter. Here we will show what happens when you roll the dice over a long period of time—examining first roll results, second roll results and additional roll results—and also look at the free-odds bets and what they can mean to a winning strategy.

HOW TO DERIVE THE BASIC ODDS FOR THE GAME OF CRAPS

For these calculations we will use the basic crap probabilities for the 36 possible combinations that a pair of dice can yield. We will also employ a large number (25,920) as the quantity of coming out rolls. A large quantity is used to eliminate the necessity for computing with a large number of decimals.

The chart shown below is a tabulation showing the calculations and probability results that would be obtained from the 25,920 coming out rolls.

FIRST ROLL RESULTS FOR 25,920 COMING OUT ROLLS				
DICE NUMBER	QUANTITY	WIN ON 1ST ROLL	LOSE ON 1ST ROLL	# OF POINTS ESTABLISHED
2	25920 x 1/36 = 720		720	
3	25920 x 2/36 = 1,440		1,440	
4	25920 x 3/36 = 2,160			2,160
5	25920 x 4/36 = 2,880			2,880
6	25920 x 5/36 = 3,600			3,600
7	25920 x 6/36 = 4,320	4,320		
8	25920 x 5/36 = 3,600			3,600
9	25920 x 4/36 = 2,880			2,880
10	25920 x 3/36 = 2,160			2,160
11	25920 x 2/36 = 1,440	1,440		
12	25920 x 1/36 = 720		720	
	Totals 25,920	5,760	2,880	17,280

From the tabulation we see that out of 25,920 coming out rolls, 5,760 winners will be produced and 2,880 losses will occur. This leaves 17,280 points whose futures are still to be decided.

On the second roll only points matched with 7's or with their own number will be retired. Those matched with 2's, 3's, 11's, 12's, or with numbers other than themselves will pass on to the third roll, since they are irrelevant to concluding the point.

The following tabulation shows results of the second roll.

RESULTS OF THE SECOND ROLL			
POINTS ESTABLISHED ON FIRST ROLL	MATCHED WITH SAME NUMBER AND RETIRED AS WINNERS	MATCHED WITH 7'S AND RETIRED AS LOSERS	CONTINUED THIRD ROLL
4's 2,160	$\frac{1440 \times 2160}{17280} = 180$	$\frac{2880 \times 2160}{17280} = 360$	1,620
5's 2,880	$\frac{1920 \times 2880}{17280} = 320$	$\frac{2880 \times 2880}{17280} = 480$	2,080
6's 3,600	$\frac{2400 \times 3600}{17280} = 500$	$\frac{2800 \times 3600}{17280} = 600$	2,500
8's 3,600	$\frac{2400 \times 3600}{17280} = 500$	$\frac{2880 \times 3600}{17280} = 600$	2,500
9's 2,880	$\frac{1920 \times 2880}{17280} = 320$	$\frac{2880 \times 2880}{17280} = 480$	2,080
10's 2,160	$\frac{1440 \times 2160}{17280} = 180$	$\frac{2880 \times 2160}{17280} = 360$	1,620
Totals 17,280	2,000	2,880	12,400

RESULTS FOR ADDITIONAL ROLLS

Results of the third roll could be computed in the same way as for the second roll, using, in this case, the 12,400 remaining points. Following this, similar computations could be made for all the additional rolls until there were no numbers left to pass on.

However, since the results of all the additional rolls would be proportional to those of the second roll, we can get the final result by establishing these proportions and multiplying them by the quantities of the points that were established by the first roll. In this way, we can construct a tabulation for all winning and losing rolls.

TABULATION OF ALL WINNING & LOSING ROLLS				
ROLL		WIN	LOSE	% OF 1ST ROLL
Winning 7's (1st roll)	25920/6	4,320		16.666
Winning 11's (1st roll)	25920/18	1,440		5.556
Losing 2's (1st roll)	25920/36		720	2.778
Losing 3's (1st roll)	25920/18		1,440	5.556
Losing 12's (1st roll)	25920/36		720	2.778
Winning 4's (w/point)	180/(180+360) X 2160	720		2.778
Winning 5's (w/point)	320/(320+480) X 2880	1,152		4.444
Winning 6's (w/point)	500/(500+600) X 3600	1,636.36		6.313
Winning 8's (w/ point)	500/(500+600) X 3600	1,636.36		6.313
Winning 9's (w/point)	320/(320+480) X 2880	1,152		4.444
Winning 10's (w/point)	180/(180+360) X 2160	720		2.778
Losing 4's (w/7)	360/(180+360) X 2160		1,440	5.556
Losing 5's (w/7)	480/(320+480) X 2880		1,728	6.666
Losing 6's (w/7)	600/(500+600) X 3600		1,963.64	7.576
Losing 8's (w/7)	600/(500+600) X 3600		1,963.64	7.576
Losing 9's (w/7)	480/(320+480) X 2800		1,728	6.666
Losing 10's (w/7)	360/(180+360) X 2160		1,440	5.556
	Totals	12,776.72	13,143.28	100.000

The results of these calculations tell us that the odds against winning when betting pass are 13,143.28 to 12,776.72. When reduced by multiplying each by the ratio of 1980/25920, we derive the odds for craps.

THE ODDS FOR CRAPS
13,143.28 x 1980/25920 = 1,004 Lose
12,776.72 x 1980/25920 = 976 Win

 # FREE ODDS BETS

After a point (4, 5, 6, 8, 9, 10) has been established on the first pass or come roll, you can place a bet of equal size to back up your bet. On a pass bet, you will place your bet behind the pass line, directly behind your bet. On a come bet, you will give your bet to the dealer, who will place it slightly off center on top of your come bet, so that it can be recognized easily as being an odds bet if the point is made and a payoff is due.

These additional bets are called odds bets, and the casino pays the correct odds on them. For example, there are three ways to roll a 4 and six ways to roll a 7. Therefore, the correct odds are 2 to 1 against the shooter rolling a 4 before he rolls a 7. Consequently, assuming a $10 bet, if a 4 is established as the point on the coming out roll and if an odds bet of $10 is placed behind the line followed by a 4 being rolled to make a winning point, the payoff would be as follows: a $10 win for the original $10 pass bet plus a $20 win for the odds bet, making a total of $30 won for $20 in bets—a total return of $50 for $20 bet.

The odds for 10 are the same as for 4; that is, 2 to 1 against making the point. The odds with 5 and 9 are 3 to 2 (four ways to roll a 5 or a 9, and six ways to roll a 7). The odds on 6 and 8 are 6 to 5 (five ways to roll a 6 or an 8 and six ways to roll a 7).

Odds bets are not contract bets. They can be picked up at any time, and can be reinstated at any time. The house will call the odds bets that have been placed on come bets off on the coming out roll of a new pass point unless instructed to keep them working.

ODDS		
NUMBER	**WAYS TO ROLL**	**ODDS**
4	3	2 to 1
5	4	3 to 2
6	5	6 to 5
8	5	6 to 5
9	4	3 to 2
10	3	2 to 1

Note: There are six ways to roll a 7, which is a loser for odds bets on the pass and come.

DOUBLE ODDS

Some casinos permit double odds. This means that you can place an odds bet that is twice as large as your pass or come bet. The payouts for these are at the same correct odds as for the single odds bets. For example, if a $10 bet had a 4 for a point and a double odds bet of $20 were placed behind the line, the return for the $30 would be $80 ($10 win on pass, plus $10 bet on pass, plus $40 win on the $20 odds bet, plus the $20 that had been bet on the odds).

Backing our pass bets with single odds bets will increase our return ratio from 98.59% to 99.15%. This means that we have decreased our loss percentage from 1.41% down to 0.85%. However, note that while you have decreased your loss percent for each roll of the dice, you have not decreased the *actual* loss.

To put it another way, you have risked more money and are no better off than if you had not added odds bets to your betting repertoire.

SINGLE ODDS RESULTS

Now let's look at what the results would have been if single odds bets had been placed behind each pass point in the five casinos:

SINGLE ODDS RESULTS FOR PASS		
	RETURN	BET
Frontier	482.40	510
Hilton	404.90	410
Caesars	811.80	809
Sands	758.40	760
Nugget	1,173.90	1,239
40-Hour Total	3,631.4	3,728.0
Return Ratio 97.41%		

Here is the math: Return (3,631.40) ÷ Amount Bet (3,728.00) x 100 = 97.41%. This appears to be an improvement over the 96.76% return ratio that betting only pass gave us.

But is it?

Let's take a look. The single pass bets resulted in a loss of 72 units (2,220 x 3.24%). Pass bets with single odds bets would have given a loss of 96.60 units (3728 x 2.59% or 3728.00 – 3631.40). Placing single odds bets behind each pass point would have resulted in a loss that was 24.60 units greater than if we had limited ourselves to single pass bets with no odds backing them.

Backing our pass bets with double odds bets will increase our probability return ratio to 99.394%, but the same will be true in this case as for single odds; no less probability loss for more money risked. The total probability bet would be 4,620 units (1980 + 1320 + 1320) which, when multiplied by the loss ratio of 0.606%, will give a loss of the same 28 units.

Now let's look at what the results would have been had double odds bets been placed behind each pass point in the five casinos.

The total bets for the 40 hours would have been $5,220. The total return would have been $5114.20. These would have given a return ratio of 97.97% (5114.20 ÷ 5220.00 x 100 = 97.97%). This is a better return ratio than the 97.41% for single odds, but the actual loss would have been 105.97 units (5,220 x 2.03% = 105.97 units), which is greater than the 96.60 units for the single odds, and 33.97 units greater loss than with no odds. This amounts to a 47% greater loss than with no odds.

	UNIT BET	UNIT PROFIT	NUMBER OF BETS	TOTAL BET	WIN	LOSE
EFFECTS OF BACKING PASS BETS WITH SINGLE ODDS BETS						
Winning 7's	1.0	1.0	4,320	4,320	4,320	
Winning 11's	1.0	1.0	1,440	1,440	1,440	
Winning 4's	2.0	3.0	720	1,440	2,160	
Winning 5's	2.0	2.5	1,152	2,304	2,880	
Winning 6's	2.0	2.2	1,636.36	3,272.72	3,599.99	
Winning 8's	2.0	2.2	1,636.36	3,272.72	3,599.99	
Winning 9's	2.0	2.5	1,152	2,304	2,880	
Winning 10's	2.0	3.0	720	1,440	2,160	
Totals				19,793.44	23,039.98	
Losing 2's	1.0		720	720		720
Losing 3's	1.0		1,440	1,440		1,440
Losing 12's	1.0		720	720		720
Losing 4's	2.0		1,440	2,880		2,880
Losing 5's	2.0		1,728	3,456		3,456
Losing 6's	2.0		1,963.64	3,927.28		3,927.28
Losing 8's	2.0		1,963.64	3,927.28		3,927.28
Losing 9's	2.0		1,728	3,456		3,456
Losing 10's	2.0		1,440	2,880		2,880
Totals				23,406.56		23,406.56

$$\frac{\text{Return}}{\text{Amount Bet}} = \frac{19{,}793.44 + 23{,}039.98}{19{,}793.44 + 23{,}406.56} \text{ x } 100 = 99.15\% \text{ Return Ratio}$$

MORE SINGLE & DOUBLE ODDS RESULTS

	UNIT BET	UNIT PROFIT	NUMBER OF BETS	TOTAL BET	WIN	LOSE
EFFECTS OF BACKING PASS BETS WITH DOUBLE ODDS BETS						
Winning 7's	1.0	1.0	4,320	4,320	4,320	
Winning 11's	1.0	1.0	1,440	1,440	1,440	
Winning 4's	3.0	5.0	720	2,160	3,600	
Winning 5's	3.0	4.0	1,152	3,456	4,608	
Winning 6's	3.0	3.4	1,636.36	4,909.08	5,563.62	
Winning 8's	3.0	3.4	1,636.36	4,909.08	5,563.62	
Winning 9's	3.0	4.0	1,152	3,456	4,608	
Winning 10's	3.0	5.0	720	2,160	3,600	
Totals				26,810.16	33,303.25	
Losing 2's	1.0		720	720		720
Losing 3's	1.0		1,440	1,440		1,440
Losing 12's	1.0		720	720		720
Losing 4's	3.0		1,440	4,320		4,320
Losing 5's	3.0		1,728	5,184		5,184
Losing 6's	3.0		1,963.64	5,890.92		5,890.92
Losing 8's	3.0		1,963.64	5,890.92		5,890.92
Losing 9's	3.0		1,728	5,184		5,184
Losing 10's	3.0		1,440	4,320		4,320
Totals				33,669.84		33,669.84

$$\frac{\text{Return}}{\text{Amount Bet}} = \frac{26,810.16 + 33,303.248}{26,810.16 + 33,669.84} \times 100 = 99.394\% \text{ Return Ratio}$$

EFFECTS OF LAYING SINGLE ODDS BETS ON ALL DON'T PASS BETS					
	UNIT BET	NUMBER OF BETS	LOSE	TOTAL BET	WIN
Losing 7's	1.0	4,320.00	4,320.00		
Losing 11's	1.0	1,440.00	1,440.00		
Losing 4's	3.0	720.00	2,160.00		
Losing 5's	2.5	1,152.00	2,880.00		
Losing 6's	2.2	1,636.36	3,599.99		
Losing 8's	2.2	1,636.36	3,599.99		
Losing 9's	2.5	1,152.00	2,880.00		
Losing 10's	3.0	720.00	2,160.00		
		Total	23,039.98		
Winning 2's	1.0	720.00		720.00	720.00
Winning 3's	1.0	1,440.00		1,440.00	1,440.00
Winning 4's	3.0	1,440.00		4,320.00	2,880.00
Winning 5's	2.5	1,728.00		4,320.00	3,456.00
Winning 6's	2.2	1,963.64		4,320.00	3,927.28
Winning 8's	2.2	1,963.64		4,320.00	3,927.28
Winning 9's	2.5	1,728.00		4,320.00	3,456.00
Winning 10's	3.0	1,440.00		4,320.00	2,880.00
		Totals		28,080.00	22,686.56

$$\frac{\text{Return}}{\text{Amount Bet}} = \frac{28,080 + 22,686.56}{23,039.984 + 28,080} \times 100 = 99.31\% \text{ Return Ratio}$$

EFFECTS OF LAYING DOUBLE ODDS BETS ON ALL DON'T PASS BETS					
	UNIT BET	NUMBER OF BETS	LOSE	TOTAL BET	WIN
Losing 7's	1.0	4,320.00	4320.00		
Losing 11's	1.0	1,440.00	1,440.00		
Losing 4's	5.0	720.00	3,600.00		
Losing 5's	4.0	1,152.00	4,608.00		
Losing 6's	3.4	1,636.36	5,563.62		
Losing 8's	3.4	1,636.36	5,563.62		
Losing 9's	4.0	1,152.00	4,608.00		
Losing 10's	5.0	720.00	3,600.00		
		Total	33,303.25		
Winning 2's	1.0	720.00		720.00	720.00
Winning 3's	1.0	1,440.00		1,440.00	1,440.00
Winning 4's	5.0	1,440.00		7,200.00	4,320.00
Winning 5's	4.0	1,728.00		6,912.00	5,184.00
Winning 6's	3.4	1,963.64		6,676.38	5,890.92
Winning 8's	3.4	1,963.64		6,676.38	5,890.92
Winning 9's	4.0	1,728.00		6,912.00	5,184.00
Winning 10's	5.0	1,440.00		7,200.00	4,320.00
		Totals		43,736.75	32,949.84

$$\frac{\text{Return}}{\text{Amount Bet}} = \frac{43{,}736.752 + 32{,}949.84}{43{,}736.752 + 33{,}303.248} \times 100 = 99.54\% \text{ Return Ratio}$$

5 COMPUTING THE PROBABILITIES FOR CONSECUTIVE EVENTS

When the probability for having something happen is known, the ratio of the whole to the number of times the event might occur is the mathematical factor used for computing multiple successive happenings. It is the successive multiplications of this factor by itself, which will yield each probability of successive happenings.

For example, for each 36 rolls of the dice the probability is that one of those rolls will be a 12. The probability says that only one 12 will appear during the 36 rolls and that there is no probability for having two 12's appear consecutively. The probability for having two consecutive 12's rolled would be once in 36 x 36 = once in 1,296 rolls. The probability of three 12's being thrown in succession would be one in 36 x 36 x 36 = or once in 46,656 rolls.

Let's consider only the case of having two successive 12's rolled. The dice, as we have computed, would have to be rolled 1,296 times in order to satisfy this probability. And during these 1,296 rolls, probability says that 36 total 12's (1,296 ÷ 36) will occur. Two of these 12's should occur back-to-back, making one consecutive situation of two 12's. Because the total number of 12's that would be rolled would be limited by probability to 36, and because two of these 12's made up the one consecutive situation of two 12's, we can reason that there would be 34 single rolls of 12 which were separated by dice numbers other than twelve.

In this case, it is easy to solve our problem by this simple logic, but when greater numbers of rolls and consecutive events are involved, simple logic will not suffice—so, let's do the calculations.

We can commence by stating that the probability for having 12 rolled is once out of each 36 rolls, and the probability for having two 12's rolled in succession is once out of 1,296 rolls. We can thus chart these:

CONSECUTIVE 12'S	
CONSECUTIVE 12'S CATEGORY	ROLLS NECESSARY TO SATISFY PROBABILITY
1	36
2	1,296

Next we can compute the maximum number that can be realized in each consecutive category by dividing the necessary rolls into the maximum number of rolls, which in this case is 1,296. We can now add another column to our chart:

CONSECUTIVE 12'S		
CONSECUTIVE CATEGORY	NECESSARY ROLLS	MAXIMUM POSSIBLE NUMBER OF COMBINATIONS IN EACH CATEGORY
1	36	36
2	1,296	1

The next step is to determine how many 12's are required for realizing all the possible categories. We can do this by multiplying the maximum possible number of combinations in each category by each consecutive category's amount. We thus add another column to our computations.

CONSECUTIVE 12'S			
CONSECUTIVE CATEGORY	NECESSARY ROLLS	MAXIMUM POSSIBLE NUMBER OF COMBINATIONS IN EACH CATEGORY	TOTAL NUMBER OF 12'S NECESSARY
1	36	36 (x 1) =	36
2	1,296	1 (x 2) =	2
		Total	38

The next step is to reduce the total calculated number of 12's to 36, which is the maximum possible number that can be realized for the 1,296 rolls of the dice. We do this by computing the percent that each possible consecutive category represents of the total, and then multiplying this percent by 36 (columns 5 and 6) in our computations.

The final step is to divide the total numbers of 12's by each category's number. This result is shown in Column 7.

CONSECUTIVE 12'S						
(1) CONSECUTIVE CATEGORY	(2) NECESSARY ROLLS	(3) MAX COMBOS EACH CATEGORY	(4) TOTAL 12'S	(5) %OF TOTAL REQUIRED 12'S	(6) TOTAL (% X 36)	(7) # IN EACH CONSECUTIVE CATEGORY
1	36	36	36	(36/38) x 100 = 94.73%	34.10	34.10
2	1,296	1	2	(2/38) x 100 = 5.27%	1.90	0.95
			Totals	100.00%	36.00	

It should be noted that our calculations show slightly less than one for the consecutive category of two 12's. This is because each consecutive category must share its total probable amount with all other consecutive categories below it. As a result, the higher the number of the consecutive category, the more will be the pressure from the categories below to reduce it from its maximum possibility.

6 PASS & DON'T PASS TABULATIONS

To demonstrate how a complex analysis is made, we will develop the calculations for the complete analysis of consecutive categories for pass, pass loss, and don't pass. The basic odds of the game of craps are 1,004 to 976 against winning. This gives a winning probability of 976 passes for each 1,980 points. This gives a probability factor for winning of $980 \div 976 = 2.03$.

The probability factor for pass bet loss is $1,980 \div 1,004 = 1.97$. With our basic odds we have 976 passes and 1,004 losses. In making our calculations we will compute to categories that are close to these basic pass and pass loss quantities.

Let us now examine a tabulation of calculations for the amounts in each pass consecutive category.

PASS & DON'T PASS TABULATIONS

CONSECUTIVE PASSES						
CONSECUTIVE PASS CATEGORY	NECESSARY ROLLS	POSSIBLE CONSECUTIVE PASSES	TOTAL POSSIBLE PASSES	% OF TOTAL PASSES	NUMBER OF PROBABLE PASSES	PROBABLE # IN EACH CONSECUTIVE PASS CATEGORY
1	2.03	582.05	582.05	25.85%	252.30	252.30
2	4.12	286.91	573.82	25.48%	248.68	124.34
3	8.35	141.42	424.27	18.84%	183.88	61.29
4	16.94	69.71	278.85	12.38%	120.83	30.21
5	34.36	34.36	171.81	7.63%	74.47	14.89
6	69.71	16.94	101.63	4.51%	44.02	7.34
7	141.42	8.35	58.45	2.60%	25.38	3.63
8	286.91	4.12	32.92	1.46%	14.25	1.78
9	582.05	2.03	18.26	0.81%	7.91	0.88
10	1,180.80	1.00	0.00	0.44%	4.29	0.43
		Totals	**2,252.06**	**100.00%**	**976.00**	

On the next page is a tabulation of calculations for the amounts in each pass loss consecutive category.

CONSECUTIVE LOSSES						
CONSECUTIVE LOSS CATEGORY	NECESSARY ROLLS	POSSIBLE CONSECUTIVE LOSSES	TOTAL POSSIBLE LOSSES	% OF TOTAL LOSSES	NUMBER OF PROBABLE LOSSES	PROBABLE # IN EACH CONSECUTIVE LOSS CATEGORY
1	1.97	451.17	451.17	24.46%	245.58	245.58
2	3.89	228.78	457.55	24.81%	249.09	124.55
3	7.67	116.01	4348.02	18.87%	189.45	63.15
4	15.1250	5882	235.30	12.76%	128.11	32.03
5	29.83	29.83	149.14	8.08%	81.12	16.22
6	58.82	15.13	90.75	4.92%	49.40	8.23
7	116.01	7.67	53.69	2.91%	29.22	4.17
8	28.78	3.89	31.11	1.69%	16.97	2.12
9	451.17	1.97	17.75	0.96%	9.64	1.07
10	889.75	1.00	10.00	0.540%	5.42	0.54
	Totals	1,844.48	100.00%	1,004.00		

In computing the quantities in each of the don't pass categories, we must return to the fundamentals of the casino game of craps, taking into account the fact that a 12 on the coming out roll is neither a win nor a loss for the don't pass bet.

Since the 12's that are present in a pass-loss category do not count as don't pass wins, the amount of the consecutive losses in any one consecutive-loss category must be reduced by the number of 12's in it to show the number of don't pass wins in that particular consecutive category.

As a result, the consecutive don't pass category that is one category number less will be increased by an amount equal to the number of 12's that were in the consecutive pass-loss category of one number higher, while at the same time having its category quantity reduced by the number of 12's originally in it.

The computations on the next page indicate how these 12's are handled and how we compute the number of consecutive don't passes in each category.

The same calculation procedure employed for computing the basic odds quantities is used for computing probable consecutive categories distributions for all other crap table bets. The only difference between calculations for each are probability factors. The total number of dice rolls will be the same for each of the 7,654 rolls of the dice that took place in the five casinos.

CONSECUTIVE DON'T PASSES

CATEGORY	# OF PASSES (PAGE 34)	# OF LOSSES (PAGE 35)	TOTAL POINTS (PASSES + LOSSES)	# OF 12'S	# IN EACH LOSS CAT. (PAGE 35)	# IN LOSS CAT LESS # OF 12'S	ADD # OF 12'S OF HIGHER CATEGORY	# IN EACH DON'T PASS CAT.	TOTAL DON'T PASSES IN EACH CAT. (CAT. X QUAN.)
1	252.2960	245.5784	497.8744	13.8299	245.5784	231.7485	13.8271	245.5756	245.5756
2	248.6848	249.0924	497.7772	13.8271	124.5462	110.7191	10.3704	121.0895	242.1790
3	183.8784	189.4548	373.3332	10.3704	63.1516	52.7812	6.9149	59.6961	179.0883
4	120.8288	128.1104	248.9392	6.9149	32.0276	25.1127	4.3220	29.4347	117.7388
5	74.4688	81.1232	155.5920	4.3220	16.2247	11.9027	2.5948	14.4975	72.4875
6	44.0176	49.3968	93.4144	2.5948	8.2328	5.6380	1.5166	7.1546	42.9276
7	25.3760	29.2164	54.5924	1.5166	4.1738	2.6572	0.8671	3.5243	24.6701
8	14.2496	16.9676	31.2172	0.8671	2.1210	1.2539	0.4873	1.7412	13.9296
9	7.9056	9.6384	17.5440	0.4873	1.0709	0.5836	0.2699	0.8535	7.6815
10	4.2944	5.4216	9.7160	0.2699	0.5421	0.2722	0.0000	0.2722	2.7220
		Totals	1,980.0000	55.0000					949.0000

7 OTHER BETS IN CRAPS

Many crap players like to place bets on the more exotic combinations of the dice. Let us examine the probabilities of several of these "enticing propositions," "enticing" being what casinos would have you believe.

FIELD & NON-FIELD

There are 16 dice combinations that produce field numbers, and 20 dice combinations producing non-field numbers, thus totaling to the 36 dice combinations. Therefore, the probability factor for consecutive field numbers is 36 ÷16 = 2.25.

For consecutive non-field numbers, it is 36 ÷ 20 = 1.8.

ANY CRAPS

Since there are only four dice combinations resulting in a crap out of 36 combinations of the dice, the probability factor for any craps is 36 ÷ 4 = 9.

2, 12, 3, 11

Since there is only one dice combination able to produce a 2, the probability factor for 2 is 36 ÷ 1 = 36. This same 36 is also the probability factor for 12.

There are two dice combinations able to produce a 3, and also only two combinations that can produce an 11. Consequently, the probability factor for both of these is 36 ÷ 2 = 18.

HARDWAY NUMBERS - 4, 10, 6, 8

The probability factor for both 4 and 10 is 9. There are three dice combinations adding to 4, and only three combinations adding to 10. Add three to the six dice combinations able to produce 7 and we have a total of nine dice positions affecting the hardway 4. And since there is only one dice position that will produce a hardway 4, the probability factor must be 9. The same is true for 10.

The probability factor for 6 and 8 is 11. There are five dice positions for 6 or 8, plus six positions for 7, with only one position for either hardway.

7

Of the 36 dice combinations, six of them can produce a 7. Therefore, the probability factor for 7 is 36 ÷ 6 = 6.

For non-7's, the probability factor is 36 ÷ 30 = 1.2.

8 PROBABLE NUMBER OF ROLLS AND DISTRIBUTIONS

Since dice is a game that is heavily involved with numbers, let us examine some further computations regarding how many rolls there might be in certain betting situations.

PROBABLE NUMBER OF ROLLS IN A PASS BET DECISION

In order to compute the probable number of dice rolls we can expect in a pass bet decision, we refer to the section where we computed odds and returns for the basic game of craps. We concluded that if there were 25,920 coming out rolls of the dice, the probability existed that there would be 17,280 second rolls and 12,400 third rolls.

Since the probability conditions during the fourth roll would be identical to those present during the second and third rolls, the number of probable rolls present in the fourth series would be in the same proportion to those of the third series as the third series was to the second. The proportion of rolls in the third series to those of the second series was 12,400 ÷ 17.280 = 0.7176. Using this ratio, we arrive at 12,400 x 0.7176 = 8,898.20 rolls for the fourth series.

If we continue this until no further rolls are possible, and then we total all the rolls for all the series, we have 87,108 rolls for the completion of the 25,920 coming out rolls. This means that the average number of rolls for each pass bet decision is 87,108 ÷ 25,920 = 3.36.

PROBABLE NUMBER OF ROLLS IN A PASS, A LOSS, AND A DON'T PASS WIN

We have determined that on the coming out rolls of the dice, there would be 5,760 7's and 11's (4,320 + 1,440), and 2,880 craps rolled for a total of 8,640 coming out rolls retired. This left 87,108 – 8,640 = 78,468 dice rolls left for completing 17,280 points starting with the second roll.

During the second roll, 2,000 passes and 2,880 losses were completed, making a total of 4,880 more points retired. Since each roll after the second retires points in the same proportion at which they were retired in the second frame, we can state that there are 78,468 x (2,000 ÷ 4,880) = 32,159 rolls that will be thrown to complete all remaining passes.

We can also say that (78,468 x 2,880) ÷ 4,880 = 46,309 rolls that will be thrown to complete all remaining losses.

Next we can compute 32,159 + 5,760 = 37,919 rolls that will be thrown for completing all pass points, which we computed as being 12,776.72. Therefore, 37,919 ÷ 12,776.72 = 2.98 rolls that will be thrown for each pass. Likewise, (46,309 + 2880 first roll craps) ÷ (13,143.28 pass losses) will be thrown for each pass loss point.

And (46,309 + 2,880) – (720 first roll 12's) ÷ (13,143.28 – 720) = 3.90 rolls that will be thrown for each don't pass win.

PROBABLE # OF ROLLS	
TYPE OF DECISION	PROBABLE # ROLLS
Pass Bet Decision	2.98
Pass Loss Decision	3.74
Pass Win Decision	3.90

HOW DICE ROLLS ARE DISTRIBUTED AMONG PASS BET DECISIONS

The probabilities for 2,220 coming out rolls say that there will be 370 7's and 123 11's for a total of 493 passes. Further, there will be 246 crap losses, of which 61½ will be 12's. This will retire 739 coming out rolls with one roll, leaving 1,481 to be retired by later rolls.

We have already concluded that of the 17,280 points left after the coming out rolls, 2,000 would be retired in the second roll as passes and 2,880 retired as losses. This gives a ratio of 2,000 ÷ 17,200 for pass retirements and 2,880 ÷ 17,280 for loss retirements.

Since conditions in the third, fourth, and all following rolls frames will be identical, we can apply these ratios for computing the pass and Loss retirements in each frame.

For example, with our 1,480 points left to be retired after the first roll, 1481 x (2,880 ÷ 17,280) = 171 points will be retired as passes in the second roll. And 1481 x (2,880 ÷ 17,280) = 247 points will be retired as losses for a total of 418 to be settled by two rolls of the dice.

This total of 418 points retired in the second roll leaves 1,481 – 418 = 1,082 points to be retired in following rolls. For example, 1,083 x (2,000 ÷ 17,280) = 125, and 1,083 x (2,880

÷ 17,280) = 180 will give us the quantities to be retired during the third roll, thus making 305 points to be completed by three rolls.

If we continue this series of calculations until the 2,220 coming out rolls have been exhausted, we will arrive at the distribution of rolls-per-point that produce the probability quantities.

PASS BET DECISIONS IN A HAND

Regardless of what combinations of what types of decisions appear in the hand, the hand ends when a 7 is rolled on any roll other than a coming out roll. A coming out roll of a 7, 11, or crap cannot be a complete hand. They can only be pass bet decisions in a hand. Therefore, whenever one of them appears on the coming out roll of a hand, the hand will automatically become one consisting of more than one pass bet decision.

The only way that a one-pass bet decision hand can be created is by having the first roll of the hand be a 4, 5, 6, 8, 9 or 10, and then have a 7 thrown in a following roll before the point number is rolled. Consequently, no hand can consist of only one roll. Therefore, a hand cannot be completed on any coming out roll. Thus the number of coming out rolls in a hand is directly equal to the number of pass bet decisions in the hand.

We have determined that out of 25,920 coming out rolls, there would be 10,263.28 losers after the coming out rolls. And since each loss could be caused only by the rolling of a 7, the 10,263.28 losses must also be the number of the hands that might result from 25,920 coming out rolls.

Therefore, the average of pass bet-decisions per hand would be 25,920 ÷ 10,263.28 = 2.52

DISTRIBUTION OF PASS BET DECISIONS IN HANDS

In computing the probability factor for points in a hand, only conditions after the coming out roll can be considered. Since there will be 17,280 points to be decided after the coming out rolls—and since 10,263.28 of these will be losers with each one being the result of a 7—the probability factor for computing this point distribution will be 17,280 ÷ 10.263.28 = 1.65.

9 INCREASING BET CALCULATIONS

When computing the results for the place bets for the three situations at the Hilton, Caesars and the Sands, I increased my bets to the maximum for each amount won. For example, if a 4 were rolled when the place bet on 4 was $5, thus giving a win of $9, I added an additional dollar to increase the bet on 4 by $10 to a bet of $15. However, my return would only be $14 dollars and not the $15 currently bet on 4 if I went "down" on my place bets at this stage.

When $15 was the place bet on 4, if a 4 was rolled, the win would be $27 and I would only increase the place bet on 4 by $25 to $40. The return in this case would now be $41. Then if another 4 were rolled, the win would be $72. But because I had a surplus of $1 on the $40 place bet, I would add $2 to be able to increase the place bet on 4 by $75 to $115. The return now would be $113. In other words, if the surplus over the $5 place bet unit is $3 or more, add the $1 or $2 required for raising the bet to the next $5 place bet unit. If the surplus is less than $3, hold the surplus for use on a later bet.

We have seen some possible results that might have been obtained from three selected situations by parlaying place bets. The calculations for these are shown on the following chart.

INCREASING BET CALCULATIONS

RETURNS FOR COMPOUNDING $5 PLACE BETS								
PLACE BET NUMBERS	**PLACE BET QUANTITIES**							
	1	**2**	**3**	**4**	**5**	**6**	**7**	**8**
4 & 10	14	41	113	320	896	2,507	7,016	16,016
5 & 9	12	26	61	145	348	838	2,014	4,835
6 & 8	13	27	62	132	286	622	1,350	2,925

HILTON		CAESARS		SANDS	
3-Fours	113	**4-Fours**	320	**5-Fours**	896
7-Fives	2,014	**3-Fives**	61	**7-Fives**	2,014
4-Sixes	132	**8-Sixes**	2,925	**5-Sixes**	286
2-Eights	27	**5-Eights**	286	**8-Eights**	2,925
7-Nines	2,014	**5-Nines**	348	**3-Nines**	61
8-Tens	16,016	**8-Tens**	16,016	**7-Tens**	7,016
Totals	**20,316**		**19,956**		**13,198**

Hilton Coming Out Rolls
4, 3, 6, 5, 11, 9, 5, 5, 10, 6

Caesars Coming Out Rolls
10, 8, 10, 2, 10, 9

Sands Coming Out Rolls
6, 10, 9, 2, 8, 6, 10, 4, 8

10 7,500 ROLLS OF THE DICE & SYSTEM TESTER WORKSHEETS

The complete data from the five casinos is tabulated in the order in which the dice produced the numbers. I recorded each roll of the dice at each casino in a notebook and later transferred the data to the data sheets reproduced on the following pages.

Each line on a data sheet shows all the rolls for competing each pass bet decision. The large number in each square shows the dice total. The small numbers in the small squares at the right show numbers on top of each die. Brackets on the left enclose all the pass bet decisions comprising each hand. To the right of each sheet is a column of small squares with the letter "W" or "L." These show whether the pass bet decisions were winners (W) or losers (L) from the viewpoint of pass betting.

If a pass bet decision had more than 16 dice rolls, it was continued on the line below. For example, if a pass bet decision had 19 dice rolls, the 17th would be recorded in the 14th square of the line below, the 18th in the 15th, and so on. The square just after the continuation would be crossed out. The pass bet decision that followed this long pass bet decision would commence at its normal location on the same line where the concluding rolls of the proceeding point has been recorded.

Notes can be added on the left side of the data sheets for any comment the player wishes to make a part of the data. For example, at Caesars I recorded the time at the conclusion of hands when the table went empty, and at the hand when play was resumed at the table. Initials at the brackets in the data from the Nugget showed hands when I rolled the dice to keep the table active.

Data presented in the form that I used for these data sheets make it easy for a person to observe how the dice performed. For that reason, I have included a blank form that you may wish to duplicate and use when testing your own system of play.

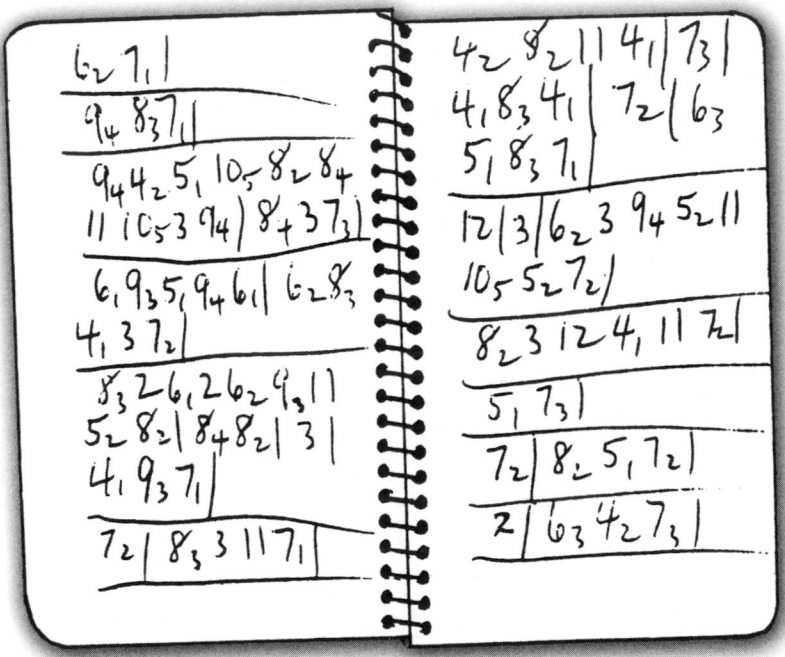

Copy of Original Notepad Used to Record Dice Rolls

_____
(Location)

Date _____   Time _____ to _____

COMING OUT	1	2	3	4	5	6	7	8	9	10	11	12	13	14	15	16	WIN or LOSS

FRONTIER HOTEL: 6/29/78 — 7:00PM – 12:30AM

COMING OUT	1	2	3	4	5	6	7	8	9	10	11	12	13	14	15	16	WIN or LOSS
4	9	6	6	6	4	4											W
9	8	4	9														W
8	4	9	10	8	4												W
9	6	3	7														L
2																	L
5	7																L
6	8	10	5	7													L
9	5	5	5	8	6	7											L
6	8	7															L
9	9																W
9	7																L
6	3	6															W
7																	W
11																	W
6	8	8	6														W
8	3	7															L
6	12	9	3	11	5	6											W
2																	L
5	9	6	6	8	6	10	8	5									W
11																	W
5	4	10	9	9	4	7											L
9	6	4	7														L
6	5	4	4	8	5	9	2	7	7								L
8	2	11	9	3	7												L
4	8	7															L
11																	W
10	5	8	6	5	7												L
5	6	10	5														W
4	4																W
5	5																W
10	11	4	6	7													L
3																	L
5	6	7															L
7																	W
6	10	7															L
8	7																L

Amount Bet									
Pass	Don't Pass	Come	Don't Come	Odds	4 or 10	5 or 9	6 or 8	Result	Total

COMING OUT	1	2	3	4	5	6	7	8	9	10	11	12	13	14	15	16	WIN or LOSS
	7																W
	7																W
	7																W
	7																W
	8	9	6	8													W
	6	8	7														L
	4	8	5	6	8	6	7										L
	7																W
	7																W
	10	8	2	5	3	6	5	7									L
	8	10	4	10	6	6	6	11	2	10	4	11	8				W
	7																W
	3																L
	12																L
	5	3	10	6	6	7											L
	4	4															W
	4	7															L
	6	9	9	12	5	9	5	10	2	10	6						W
	9	10	8	11	6	7											L
	5	7															L
	8	7															L
	9	11	3	2	8	3	8	11	7								L
	8	8															W
	6	10	6														W
	10	9	6	8	3	5	11	11	7								L
	9	8	8	10	6	11	10	8	7								L
	8	5	9	6	10	6	8										W
	3																L
	7																W
	2																L
	6	5	5	6													W
	10	6	2	7													L
	2																L
	7																W
	7																W
	5	10	10	4	7												L

	Amount Bet								
Pass	Don't Pass	Come	Don't Come	Odds	4 or 10	5 or 9	6 or 8	Result	Total

FRONTIER HOTEL: 6/29/78 — 7:00PM – 12:30AM

1 COMING OUT	2	3	4	5	6	7	8	9	10	11	12	13	14	15	16	WIN or LOSS
6 3/3	7 1/6															L
3 1/2																L
7 1/6																W
8 4/4	6 2/4	10 4/6	8 3/5													W
5 2/3	5 1/4															W
9 3/6	6 1/5	9 4/5														W
8 2/6	6 2/4	9 3/6	8 4/4													W
8 2/6	10 5/5	7 1/6														L
3 1/2																L
8 3/5	8 2/6															W
10 4/6	10 4/6															W
6 2/4	7 1/6															L
5 2/3	6 2/4	4 2/2	9 3/6	2 1/1	7 3/4											L
10 5/5	8 3/5	9 4/5	10 4/6													W
9 4/5	9 3/6															W
4 1/3	7 1/6															L
7 3/4																W
8 4/4	10 5/5	6 2/4	7 2/5													L
8 2/6	7 2/4															L
11 5/6																W
12 6/6																L
7 1/6																W
6 1/5	3 1/2	4 1/3	9 3/6	7 1/6												L
9 4/5	5 1/4	8 2/6	4 1/3	11 5/6	6 2/4	8 3/5	9 4/5									W
12 6/6																L
3 1/2																L
7 1/6																W
6 1/5	9 4/5	12 6/6	12 6/6	10 4/6	7 1/6											L
7 3/4																W
11 5/6																W
7 2/5																W
7 1/6																W
9 4/5	5 2/3	9 3/6														W
3 1/2																L
7 2/5																W
9 4/5	7 2/5															L

					Amount Bet				
Pass	Don't Pass	Come	Don't Come	Odds	4 or 10	5 or 9	6 or 8	Result	Total

COMING OUT	2	3	4	5	6	7	8	9	10	11	12	13	14	15	16	WIN or LOSS
7 3/6																W
8 4/6	5 2/5	10 4/6	12 6/6	9 3/6	4 2/2	3 1/1	12 2/6	7 1/6								L
8 3/6	3 1/2	4 1/5	10 4/6	9 1/6	5 2/6	7 1/6										L
7 2/6																W
6 1/5	12 6/6	6 3/5														W
4 4/6	4 2/2															W
3 1/1																L
8 2/6	5 1/4	2 1/1	3 2/4	7 2/4												L
10 4/6	3 2/6	5 1/4	5 4/6	7 2/6												L
6 3/5	9 2/6	7 1/6														L
10 4/6	9 3/6	8 2/5	12 4/6	10 4/6												W
6 4/6	6 3/5															W
9 4/6	6 2/4	12 6/6	11 5/6	10 5/6	12 4/6	5 1/4	6 3/5	5 2/4	9 4/5							W
6 4/6	7 1/6															L
8 3/6	9 4/5	9 4/5	2 1/1	8 3/5												W
8 3/6	5 2/6	6 2/5	3 1/4	4 2/2	6 2/4	2 1/1	4 2/2	2 1/1	3 2/6	6 1/5	6 3/6	6 2/4	4 3/4	4 2/2	5 2/5	W
12 6/6												▨	5 1/4	10 4/6	8 2/5	L
6 1/5	5 2/3	9 3/6	9 4/6	9 4/6	10 5/6	4 2/4	8 3/5	6 1/5								W
6 4/6	6 3/5															W
12 6/6																L
7 4/6																W
6 4/6	11 5/6	10 5/6	10 4/6	4 1/3	8 2/6	10 4/6	5 2/3	9 4/6	7 3/4							L
5 2/6	10 4/6	9 3/6	7 2/5													L
6 3/5	9 2/6	7 4/6														L
9 3/6	11 5/6	8 3/5	11 5/6	6 4/6	5 2/3	7 1/6										L
11 5/6																W
8 2/6	8 3/5															W
4 2/6	7 3/4															L
3 1/2																L
2 1/1																L
5 1/4	10 4/6	6 3/5	5 4/4													W
8 4/6	10 5/6	8 3/5														W
2 1/1																L
10 4/6	9 4/5	10 4/6														W
8 2/6	7 1/6															L
8 2/6	9 4/5	7 2/6														L

Amount Bet									
Pass	Don't Pass	Come	Don't Come	Odds	4 or 10	5 or 9	6 or 8	Result	Total

COMING OUT 1	2	3	4	5	6	7	8	9	10	11	12	13	14	15	16	WIN or LOSS
7																W
5	5															W
4	10	12	7													L
8	9	7														L
5	9	10	8	8	8	10	8	7								L
5	5															W
7																W
8	10	3	7													L
6	8	10	9	12	7											L
4	12	9	7													L
9	4	10	5	5	8	7										L
11																W
5	2	3	9	5												W
6	7															L
3																L
6	6															W
6	4	6														W
5	8	5														W
6	9	7														L
8	8															W
9	9															W
6	4	7														L
8	6	10	2	8												W
5	6	12	10	10	8	7										L
8	10	4	8													W
5	6	11	8	6	10	4	10	5								W
11																W
6	11	9	6													W
6	6															W
4	6	8	7													L
9	6	6	7													L
9	7															L
7																W
7																W
6	6															W
4	8	5	5	9	9	11	7									L

Amount Bet									
Pass	Don't Pass	Come	Don't Come	Odds	4 or 10	5 or 9	6 or 8	Result	Total

COMING OUT 1	2	3	4	5	6	7	8	9	10	11	12	13	14	15	16	WIN or LOSS
8²⁄₆	8²⁄₆															W
6²⁄₄	9³⁄₄	11	12⁵⁄₆	8³⁄₅	5¹⁄₄	8³⁄₅	10⁵⁄₅	6¹⁄₅								W
8²⁄₆	7²⁄₅															L
7³⁄₄																W
4²⁄₂	5³⁄₄	3¹⁄₂	7⁴⁄₆													L
8²⁄₆	4⁴⁄₃	7³⁄₄														L
7¹⁄₆																W
9²⁄₆	7²⁄₄															L
10⁵⁄₅	6¹⁄₃	7²⁄₄														L
11⁵⁄·																W
10⁵⁄₄	4³⁄₅	4³⁄₄	7²⁄₃													L
2¹⁄₁																L
7¹⁄₆																W
11⁴⁄₆																W
8²⁄₆	5²⁄₃	7²⁄₅														L
7³⁄₄																W
9²⁄₆	5²⁄₃	8²⁄₆	7²⁄₅													L
6¹⁄₃	4²⁄₄	10⁴⁄₆	7⁴⁄₄													L
4²⁄₂	3¹⁄₂	7⁴⁄₆														L
7¹⁄₆																W
2¹⁄₁																L
3¹⁄₂																L
7²⁄₆																W
6²⁄₄	5²⁄₃	5²⁄₂	7⁴⁄₆													L
3¹⁄₁																L
11⁵⁄·																W
9³⁄₃	7²⁄₅															L
8³⁄₅	8³⁄₅															W
5⁴⁄₆	8²⁄₆	3²⁄₂	3²⁄₂	4³⁄₅	9⁴⁄₂	12⁴⁄₆	2¹⁄₁	7³⁄₂								L
6⁴⁄₄	4³⁄₅	2¹⁄₁	8⁴⁄₆	8³⁄₅	5²⁄₃	6⁴⁄₄										W
8⁴⁄₅	5²⁄₃	4³⁄₂	8²⁄₆													W
6²⁄₄	3¹⁄₂	9³⁄₆	8²⁄₆	7³⁄₃												L
7¹⁄₄																W
5⁴⁄₃	6²⁄₄	7²⁄₂														L
7²⁄₆																W
8²⁄₆	8⁴⁄₄															W

Amount Bet								Result	Total
Pass	Don't Pass	Come	Don't Come	Odds	4 or 10	5 or 9	6 or 8	Result	Total

FRONTIER HOTEL: 6/29/78 — 7:00PM — 12:30AM

COMING OUT	2	3	4	5	6	7	8	9	10	11	12	13	14	15	16	WIN or LASS
10	9	6	6	7												L
3																L
5	7															L
5	5															W
7																W
9	6	8	8	6	6	9										W
8	8															W
6	4	3	4	4	4	8	6	6								W
6	8	12	7													L
9	11	7														L
6	4	8	8	10	6											W
9	10	5	4	3	7											L
5	11	2	10	6	5											W
8	9	3	12	9	10	10	8									W
8	6	10	10	11	6	2	5	8								W
8	7															L
4	7															L
3																L
5	7															L
6	9	4	7													L
5	10	8	9	7												L
5	7															L
4	3	8	9	9	8	8	9	5	5	11	8	7				L
8	9	6	11	5	10	6	7									L
6	5	9	12	9	8	3	4	5	7							L
4	5	6	9	8	3	10	6	8	3	11	5	7				L
8	12	3	10	10	9	7										L
10	4	11	5	9	6	6	6	8	4	4	6	3	8	6	8	L
4	9	9	5	6	8	12	8	6	7					7		L
3																L
9	8	7														L
8	6	5	9	3	8											W
6	7															L
5	6	4	7													L
10	6	7														L
11																W

64

					4 or 10	5 or 9	6 or 8		
				Amount Bet					
Pass	Don't Pass	Come	Don't Come	Odds	4 or 10	5 or 9	6 or 8	Result	Total

COMING OUT	1	2	3	4	5	6	7	8	9	10	11	12	13	14	15	16	WIN or LOSS
	5	10	8	8	8	8	12	3	7	7							L
	5	4	11	6	6	6	5										W
	10	7															L
	3																L
	7																W
	5	5															W
	8	6	3	6	9	6	10	5	6	6	7						L
	10	6	11	9	9	8	5	9	3	5	8	9	7				L
	8	10	10	6	5	7											L
	9	8	9														W
	10	3	9	7													L
	6	8	12	8	7												L
	4	5	10	8	8	4											W
	4	8	8	9	8	9	4										W
	3																L
	7																W
	4	8	10	3	12	4											W
	6	6															W
	8	6	12	8													W
	11																W
	3																L
	11																W
	6	2	5	6													W
	6	7															L
	10	7															L
	10	6	6	9	12	4	7										L
	5	4	7														L
	5	8	8	4	7												L
	8	8															W
	7																W
	8	11	9	10	6	3	5	7									L
	7																W
	5	8	8	9	3	8	6	7									L
	10	8	9	4	7												L
	5	11	4	7													L
	5	7															L

				Amount Bet					
Pass	Don't Pass	Come	Don't Come	Odds	4 or 10	5 or 9	6 or 8	Result	Total

FRONTIER HOTEL: 6/29/78 — 7:00PM – 12:30AM

COMING OUT	1	2	3	4	5	6	7	8	9	10	11	12	13	14	15	16	WIN or LOSS
8	11	6	10	7	7												L
9	5	6	2	8	10	10	6	9									W
12																	L
9	8	9															W
6	7																L
10	8	5	8	10													W
8	6	2	4	9	8												W
6	5	3	10	12	10	7											L
2																	L
2																	L
10	8	6	7														L

68

	Amount Bet								
Pass	Don't Pass	Come	Don't Come	Odds	4 or 10	5 or 9	6 or 8	Result	Total

COMING OUT 1	2	3	4	5	6	7	8	9	10	11	12	13	14	15	16	WIN or LOSS
6	8	7														L
10	6	7														L
6	4	4	8	6												W
10	8	8	3	4	4	12	8	6	5	4	6	5	10			W
6	6															W
12																L
5	7															L
3																L
5	7															L
5	5															W
5	6	6	11	8	5											W
6	10	3	11	11	8	2	10	12	4	10	11	5	7			L
5	9	9	7													L
4	10	6	12	9	7											L
10	6	10														W
9	7															L
10	7															L
9	9															W
6	11	8	5	9	3	3	8	5	11	6						W
9	7															L
8	10	11	6	12	6	4	6	7								L
4	9	4														W
7																W
10	6	6	2	8	10											W
7																W
8	9	9	10	7												L
6	4	2	12	4	10	8	8	7								L
10	4	6	6	12	5	5	6	11	8	3	8	8	9	8	3	L
7													5	7		W
4	12	12	8	6	7											L
8	4	7														L
7																W
10	8	5	6	6	8	6	8	4	9	4	11	6	5	9	4	L
8	8						11	5	11	2	5	8	7			W
7																W
8	5	7														L

Amount Bet									
Pass	Don't Pass	Come	Don't Come	Odds	4 or 10	5 or 9	6 or 8	Result	Total

HILTON: 6/30/78 — 8:00PM – 1:00AM

COMING OUT																	WIN or LOSS
1	2	3	4	5	6	7	8	9	10	11	12	13	14	15	16		
5	11	10	9	2	5												W
6	4	9	10	8	6												W
3																	L
5	7																L
10	4	3	7														L
2																	L
6	9	4	8	11	4	7											L
9	9																W
6	7																L
8	11	12	2	5	3	5	8										W
5	12	3	8	6	5												W
5	8	8	4	8	8	6	10	3	5								W
8	9	4	4	5	5	9	7										L
5	5																W
6	6																W
5	8	9	5														W
8	8																W
9	5	11	5	6	3	6	11	5	6	4	7						L
8	7																L
8	6	3	7														L
4	9	5	8	8	11	11	2	7	7								L
10	3	8	7														L
8	8																W
7																	W
2																	L
6	9	7															L
9	8	5	10	7													L
5	3	7															L
6	6																W
6	6																W
11																	W
5	10	2	6	5													W
5	6	7															L
4	4																W
10	10																W
6	8	10	7														L

72

					4 or 10	5 or 9	6 or 8	Result	Total
			Amount Bet						
Pass	Don't Pass	Come	Don't Come	Odds					

HILTON: 6/30/78 — 8:00PM — 1:00AM

COMING OUT	2	3	4	5	6	7	8	9	10	11	12	13	14	15	16	WIN or LOSS
6	10	4	3	7												L
12																L
9	6	8	4	7												L
7																W
9	11	12	7													L
5	4	7														L
4	6	6	9	8	7											L
8	8															W
9	7															L
6	9	11	7													L
5	11	8	7													L
6	6															W
6	7															L
3																L
8	4	7														L
8	8															W
6	6															W
7																W
6	3	5	8	9	4	11	7									L
7																W
9	2	2	7													L
4	4															W
7																W
3																L
9	9															W
3																L
5	8	8	10	4	7											L
11																W
11																W
6	2	4	8	9	11	10	7									L
6	8	6														W
12																L
6	11	9	5	6												W
6	10	8	4	11	5	4	4	7								L
5	9	2	2	8	10	12	11	6	8	11	5					W
9	2	5	7													L

74

			Amount Bet						
Pass	Don't Pass	Come	Don't Come	Odds	4 or 10	5 or 9	6 or 8	Result	Total

COMING OUT	2	3	4	5	6	7	8	9	10	11	12	13	14	15	16	WIN or LOSS
4	5	7														L
5	6	4	2	11	10	6	8	11	6	6	5	5				W
8	10	12	9	7												L
7																W
10	5	10														W
7																W
6	9	9	7													L
5	7															L
5	8	2	8	6	5											W
10	9	3	8	6	6	5	5	11	8	6	3	8	10			W
5	4	9	6	7												L
7																W
4	9	9	3	9	7											L
5	9	6	4	8	9	12	7									L
9	9															W
3																L
9	7															L
9	9															W
4	11	3	6	6	6	8	7									L
5	12	8	10	8	9	10	9	4	10	3	5					W
4	4															W
9	2	7														L
10	8	8	6	11	8	10										W
7																W
8	6	3	10	11	8											W
7																W
10	12	9	12	12	7											L
5	8	7														L
5	12	6	7													L
11																W
6	7															L
9	8	9														W
6	8	10	2	10	7											L
10	6	11	8	11	8	4	8	7								L
3																L
5	10	9	11	3	11	8	11	3	3	7						L

76

			Amount Bet						
Pass	Don't Pass	Come	Don't Come	Odds	4 or 10	5 or 9	6 or 8	Result	Total

COMING OUT 1	2	3	4	5	6	7	8	9	10	11	12	13	14	15	16	WIN or LOSS
5	12	5														W
10	4	9	5	2	7											L
10	4	3	6	8	4	9	11	8	8	7						L
2																L
4	3	5	10	9	7											L
10	12	4	9	9	9	5	11	7								L
10	3	6	12	4	7											L
6	12	5	5	8	5	8	7									L
10	7															L
10	8	9	5	4	2	8	9	8	6	9	7					L
11																W
7																W
12																L
4	9	8	9	11	6	8	7									L
3																L
3																L
9	8	3	8	10	6	8	2	7								L
11																W
10	6	9	7													L
6	6															W
5	11	6	6	7												L
4	7															L
3																L
11																W
7																W
10	4	5	7													L
10	7															L
3																L
7																W
4	6	8	8	4												W
6	10	6														W
6	5	6														W
4	4															W
7																W
7																W
8	10	2	4	7												L

				Amount Bet					
Pass	Don't Pass	Come	Don't Come	Odds	4 or 10	5 or 9	6 or 8	Result	Total

HILTON: 6/30/78 — 8:00PM – 1:00AM

COMING OUT																WIN or LOSS
1	2	3	4	5	6	7	8	9	10	11	12	13	14	15	16	
12																L
4	6	6	6	11	3	3	2	6	7	7						L
6	9	11	6													W
4	6	6	6	11	6	11	10	8	5	8	5	6	8	3	7	L
6	2	7														L
9	3	7														L
6	7															L
5	5															W
6	8	7														L
5	9	10	7													L
9	8	7														L
6	4	2	3	11	5	4	6									W
11																W
8	10	7														L
5	9	5														W
5	8	2	10	9	8	2	10	10	9	3	6	6	4	3	8	W
2										12	10	8	2	11	5	L
6	3	4	6													W
8	8															W
3																L
5	9	7														L
7																W
11																W
4	10	10	6	6	9	5	4	4								W
8	2	6	7													L
7																W
5	8	10	10	7												L
7																W
7																W
6	8	3	7													L
5	7															L
9	2	8	5	9												W
11																W
4	5	7														L
4	4															W
3																L

		Amount Bet							
Pass	Don't Pass	Come	Don't Come	Odds	4 or 10	5 or 9	6 or 8	Result	Total

COMING OUT	1	2	3	4	5	6	7	8	9	10	11	12	13	14	15	16	WIN or LOSS
	6	8	9	9	9	3	11	9	6	6							W
	5	4	6	5													W
	11																W
	9	10	5	9													W
	5	10	3	10	11	5											W
	5	10	9	10	10	5											W
	10	8	9	10													W
	6	7															L
	6	6															W
	7																W
	9	8	7														L
	9	8	7														L
	5	3	10	4	5	5											W
	5	7															L
	9	5	9														W
	5	9	6	5													W
	9	9															W
	6	11	12	7													L

GAMBLER'S BOOK CLUB **THOMAS MIDGLEY**

					4 or 10	5 or 9	6 or 8		
Pass	Don't Pass	Come	Don't Come	Odds				Result	Total

Amount Bet

COMING OUT 1	2	3	4	5	6	7	8	9	10	11	12	13	14	15	16	WIN or LOSS
3																L
9	3	6	8	4	9											W
4	6	11	12	8	8	8	10	8	7							L
6	7															L
2																L
8	7															L
10	3	4	10													W
8	11	8														W
6	10	5	10	9	9	6										W
6	7															L
6	8	3	9	7												L
8	12	8														W
4	9	5	11	5	6	8	8	8	10	4						W
7																W
7																W
2																L
4	4															W
11																W
5	8	6	8	9	5											W
4	2	11	9	6	10	8	5	4								W
7																W
7																W
8	8															W
8	6	3	7													L
7																W
9	10	10	6	10	7											L
6	3	9	7													L
9	2	5	3	10	9											W
10	6	4	5	10												W
7																W
11																W
7																W
11																W
11																W
4	9	4														W
8	9	7														L

Amount Bet									
Pass	Don't Pass	Come	Don't Come	Odds	4 or 10	5 or 9	6 or 8	Result	Total

CAESAR'S: 10/17/78 — 4:00PM – 2:00AM

1 COMING OUT	2	3	4	5	6	7	8	9	10	11	12	13	14	15	16	WIN or LOSS
9 3/6	6 1/5	4 1/3	7 2/5													L
7 2/5																W
9 4/5	9 3/6															W
12 6/6																L
4 1/3	9 3/6	6 1/5	8 4/4	4 1/3												W
5 1/4	6 2/4	6 2/4	7 1/6													L
5 2/3	7 2/5															L
7 3/4																W
9 3/6	8 3/5	6 1/5	7 3/4													L
3 1/2																L
8 3/5	6 1/5	5 2/3	11 5/6	2 1/1	9 3/6	9 3/6	10 5/5	7 3/4								L
8 4/4	6 3/3	5 1/4	9 3/6	9 3/6	7 2/5											L
8 3/5	6 3/3	2 1/1	7 3/4													L
8 2/6	8 2/6															W
6 1/5	4 2/2	7 2/5														L
5 2/3	4 2/2	6 2/4	8 2/6	8 3/5	7 1/6											L
10 4/6	7 3/4															L
4 1/3	4 2/2															W
7 1/6																W
6 3/3	8 3/5	9 3/6	9 3/6	7 2/5												L
8 2/6	8 2/6															W
7 3/4																W
4 1/3	7 2/5															L
7 1/6																W
7 2/5																W
7 3/4																W
4 1/3	7 1/6															L
8 4/4	12 6/6	9 4/5	5 2/3	6 1/5	7 1/6											L
6 2/4	8 2/6	6 2/4														W
5 2/3	6 2/4	7 2/5														L
7 1/6																W
9 4/5	5 1/4	9 4/5														W
6 2/4	7 2/5															L
5 2/3	8 2/6	7 1/6														L
7 2/5																W
5 2/3	6 1/5	8 2/6	9 3/6	8 2/6	7 1/6											L

					Amount Bet				
Pass	Don't Pass	Come	Don't Come	Odds	4 or 10	5 or 9	6 or 8	Result	Total

COMING OUT	2	3	4	5	6	7	8	9	10	11	12	13	14	15	16	WIN or LOSS
4	3	7														L
11																W
2																L
7																W
5	8	6	9	7												L
5	12	11	10	10	4	9	7	7								L
7																W
7																W
5	5															W
7																W
4	7															L
3																L
11																W
5	6	10	7													L
7																W
4	12	11	7													L
2																L
11																W
7																W
5	10	6	2	10	6	7										L
7																W
7																W
7																W
8	7															L
3																L
6	7															L
9	5	11	2	9												W
7																W
11																W
6	8	5	3	6												W
5	12	6	8	4	7											L
5	7															L
5	10	11	10	12	7											L
6	7															L
3																L
10	3	4	9	7												L

Amount Bet									
Pass	Don't Pass	Come	Don't Come	Odds	4 or 10	5 or 9	6 or 8	Result	Total

COMING OUT 1	2	3	4	5	6	7	8	9	10	11	12	13	14	15	16	WIN or LOSS
7																W
6	8	8	4	4	4	7										L
8	6	8														W
4	7															L
10	7															L
3																L
4	8	6	8	8	9	7										L
8	9	7														L
4	6	9	6	6	10	7										L
11																W
3																L
8	5	6	3	9	6	7										L
6	7															L
7																W
3																L
2																L
3																L
8	7															L
9	10	8	7													L
10	8	6	5	6	8	3	9	5	8	9	10					W
6	7															L
6	11	8	9	7												L
9	9															W
10	4	10														W
9	10	11	4	11	10	5	5	4	7							L
6	12	8	11	7												L
11																W
6	6															W
8	6	9	8													W
8	8															W
9	7															L
12																L
7																W
3																L
2																L
6	9	9	10	10	5	5	2	6								W

					4 or 10	5 or 9	6 or 8		
			Amount Bet						
Pass	Don't Pass	Come	Don't Come	Odds	4 or 10	5 or 9	6 or 8	Result	Total

COMING OUT 1	2	3	4	5	6	7	8	9	10	11	12	13	14	15	16	WIN or LOSS
8	6	5	7	7												L
4	10	8	9	10	3	2	8	7								L
4	7															L
8	10	5	9	2	11	8										W
5	10	7														L
11																W
6	7															L
6	5	10	5	9	6											W
6	5	8	4	7												L
3																L
2																L
7																W
9	6	10	4	4	7											L
7																W
8	8															W
3																L
6	11	8	6													W
9	3	4	3	8	4	3	9									W
7																W
7																W
5	7															L
4	5	2	4													W
7																W
4	7															L
5	5															W
10	4	4	7													L
4	9	7														L
9	4	9														W
4	7															L
9	10	5	10	6	10	8	3	4	2	9						W
6	5	8	5	7												L
7																W
8	2	4	3	8												W
9	4	4	6	10	5	5	10	5	9							W
9	8	5	3	5	5	5	9									W
9	7															L

92

Amount Bet									
Pass	Don't Pass	Come	Don't Come	Odds	4 or 10	5 or 9	6 or 8	Result	Total

CAESAR'S: 10/17/78 — 4:00PM – 2:00AM

COMING OUT	1	2	3	4	5	6	7	8	9	10	11	12	13	14	15	16	WIN or LOSS
$5\frac{2}{3}$	$5\frac{1}{4}$																W
$2\frac{4}{4}$																	L
$4\frac{2}{2}$	$5\frac{1}{4}$	$6\frac{2}{4}$	$10\frac{5}{5}$	$7\frac{1}{5}$													L
$2\frac{4}{4}$																	L
$3\frac{4}{2}$																	L
$12\frac{6}{6}$																	L
$3\frac{4}{4}$																	L
$7\frac{4}{6}$																	W
$7\frac{1}{4}$																	W
$7\frac{3}{5}$																	W
$10\frac{5}{5}$	$7\frac{3}{4}$																L
$7\frac{6}{6}$																	W
$6\frac{4}{4}$	$8\frac{1}{4}$	$10\frac{5}{6}$	$5\frac{5}{3}$	$8\frac{1}{4}$	$9\frac{4}{3}$	$7\frac{3}{4}$											L
$7\frac{6}{6}$																	W
$5\frac{2}{3}$	$5\frac{2}{3}$																W
$7\frac{2}{5}$																	W
$8\frac{2}{4}$	$11\frac{5}{6}$	$9\frac{4}{5}$	$5\frac{1}{4}$	$7\frac{1}{6}$													L
$11\frac{5}{6}$																	W
$7\frac{1}{4}$																	W
$12\frac{4}{6}$																	L
$3\frac{4}{4}$																	L
$3\frac{1}{2}$																	L
$7\frac{4}{2}$																	W
$7\frac{2}{5}$																	W
$6\frac{1}{5}$	$9\frac{4}{5}$	$7\frac{3}{4}$															L
$10\frac{4}{4}$	$7\frac{2}{5}$																L
$4\frac{1}{3}$	$7\frac{3}{4}$																L
$6\frac{1}{5}$	$9\frac{4}{5}$	$7\frac{1}{6}$															L
$5\frac{1}{4}$	$7\frac{1}{6}$																L
$9\frac{4}{5}$	$5\frac{2}{3}$	$5\frac{1}{4}$	11	$5\frac{5}{4}$	$10\frac{4}{6}$	$6\frac{3}{4}$	$4\frac{1}{3}$	11	$8\frac{5}{3}$	$9\frac{3}{4}$							W
$7\frac{3}{4}$																	W
$4\frac{1}{3}$	$6\frac{2}{4}$	$7\frac{2}{5}$															L
$11\frac{5}{5}$																	W
$10\frac{5}{5}$	$3\frac{1}{2}$	$7\frac{3}{4}$															L
$11\frac{5}{5}$																	W
$8\frac{2}{6}$	$6\frac{4}{4}$	$2\frac{4}{4}$	4	$3\frac{4}{5}$	$12\frac{6}{6}$	$4\frac{4}{2}$	$7\frac{3}{4}$										L

94

Amount Bet								Result	Total
Pass	Don't Pass	Come	Don't Come	Odds	4 or 10	5 or 9	6 or 8	Result	Total

CAESAR'S: 10/17/78 — 4:00PM – 2:00AM

1 COMING OUT	2	3	4	5	6	7	8	9	10	11	12	13	14	15	16	WIN or LOSS
4 1/3	3 1/2	6 1/5	12 6/6	6 2/4	8 3/5	4 1/3										W
7 1/6																W
8 2/6	8 2/6															W
2 1/1																L
9 3/6	4 2/2	7 1/6														L
9 3/6	2 1/1	11 5/6	7 2/5													L
8 2/5	3 1/2	8 2/5														W
8 2/6	8 3/5															W
6 2/3	7 3/4															L
6 2/4	7 2/5															L
3 1/2																L
7 1/6																W
9 3/6	10 4/6	7 3/4														L
5 1/4	2 1/1	11 5/6	9 3/6	9 4/5	4 2/2	9 4/5	3 1/2	7 1/6								L
5 2/3	6 2/4	5 2/3														W
8 4/4	7 2/5															L
6 3/3	8 3/5	4 1/3	6 2/4													W
5 2/3	6 1/5	8 3/5	4 2/2	9 3/6	8 3/5	7 3/4										L
7 1/6																W
7 1/6																W
6 2/4	7 2/5															L
7 3/4																W
9 3/6	4 1/3	5 2/3	7 2/5													L
7 3/4																W
6 3/4	4 1/3	6 1/5														W
7 2/5																W
10 5/5	6 2/4	6 3/3	10 4/6													W
8 3/3	7 1/6															L
8 4/4	5 2/3	7 2/5														L
3 1/2																L
9 3/6	4 2/2	4 1/3	7 3/4													L
8 4/4	4 2/2	10 4/6	6 1/5	6 1/5	6 1/5	10 5/5	6 2/4	5 1/4	8 2/5							W
9 3/6	4 1/3	8 2/6	8 3/5	9 3/6												W
6 1/5	5 1/4	5 2/3	5 2/3	7 1/6												L
3 1/2																L
6 1/5	10 5/5	9 4/5	5 2/3	6 1/5												W

				Amount Bet					
Pass	Don't Pass	Come	Don't Come	Odds	4 or 10	5 or 9	6 or 8	Result	Total

COMING OUT	1	2	3	4	5	6	7	8	9	10	11	12	13	14	15	16	WIN or LOSS
	11 5/6																W
	9 2/3	7 3/4															L
	3 3/4																L
	4 5/6	5 1/4	5 1/3	8 4/4	3 1/4	7 2/5											L
	5 1/4	6 3/4	5 2/3														W
	7 1/6																W
	3 3/4																L
	8 5/6	7 4/6															L
	2 1/4																L
	6 1/5	8 5/6	8 2/3	5 2/3	8 3/5	10 4/4	8 2/5	9 3/6	8 5/6	5 2/3	10 5/4	4	2	9 4/4	4 1/3	5 1/4	W
	6 3/4	2	7	7 1/4									▨	8 2/6	10 4/6	6 2/5	L
	7 2/6																W
	7 1/6																W
	8 3/5	9 4/6	8 3/5														W
	8 3/5	3 4/6	8 3/5														W
	5 4/6	2	7 4/6														L
	9 4/5	8 2/6	7 2/5														L
	7 1/6																W
	7 2/6																W
	10 4/6	9 3/6	5 3/4	10 5/5													W
	5 4/6	8 3/4	7 1/6														L
	4 1/6	7 3/4															L
	6 4/6	11	9 4/5	6 1/3													W
	8 2/5	8 4/6															W
	4 2/6	9 3/6	8 3/6	11 5/6	11	4 2/6	4 2/2										W
	5 4/6	9 3/6	9 4/6	9 3/6	8 5/6	4 1/3	9 4/4	3	11 5/6	4 4/3	5 1/4						W
	8 2/6	7 4/6															L
	7 2/6																W
	9 3/6	4 1/3	7 1/3														L
	12 4/6																L
	11 5/6																W
	7 4/6																W
	7 1/6																W
	9 3/6	10 4/6	5 2/3	5 2/3	6 2/4	7 2/5											L
	9 4/6	5 2/3	4 2/3	9 4/3													W
	8 3/5	4 1/3	5 3/5	8 4/4													W

Amount Bet									
Pass	Don't Pass	Come	Don't Come	Odds	4 or 10	5 or 9	6 or 8	Result	Total

COMING OUT	1	2	3	4	5	6	7	8	9	10	11	12	13	14	15	16	WIN or LOSS
6	8	9	8	8	6												W
11																	W
6	4	6															W
6	7																L
9	7																L
10	7																L
11																	W
7																	W
4	6	3	5	10	9	11	8	7									L
10	9	2	9	4	8	8	9	8	6	3	10						W
3																	L
4	9	3	8	8	4												W
9	4	10	8	6	7												L
10	5	9	8	7													L
9	7																L
7																	W
7																	W
6	5	7															L
11																	W
3																	L
8	4	10	8														W
7																	W
4	4																W
11																	W
11																	W
11																	W
10	10																W
9	8	10	9														W
4	6	7															L
7																	W
4	6	10	4														W
3																	L
7																	W
8	8																W
7																	W
3																	L
8	5	7															L

Amount Bet								Result	Total
Pass	Don't Pass	Come	Don't Come	Odds	4 or 10	5 or 9	6 or 8	Result	Total

COMING OUT 1	2	3	4	5	6	7	8	9	10	11	12	13	14	15	16	WIN or LOSS
6	5	5	7													L
7																W
9	6	3	7													L
5	9	4	7													L
7																W
7																W
5	7															L
4	5	12	8	7												L
9	3	6	8	7												L
10	6	9	5	8	11	10										W
8	2	3	6	11	6	8										W
10	3	9	11	10												W
2																L
10	5	6	9	4	8	6	4	10								W
9	10	6	6	4	5	8	10	4	6	9						W
7																W
9	10	7														L
4	7															L
5	7															L
3																L
10	9	5	6	4	4	7										L
4	6	7														L
8	7															L
10	8	11	11	7												L
7																W
7																W
7																W
4	9	12	4													W
10	6	12	6	6	9	5	8	8	4	2	12	11	9	3	9	W
9	7						5	9	6	4	4	6	12	10		L
7																W
7																W
10	7															L
8	3	7														L
6	5	6														W
6	8	9	11	4	10	7										L

Amount Bet									
Pass	Don't Pass	Come	Don't Come	Odds	4 or 10	5 or 9	6 or 8	Result	Total

COMING OUT 1	2	3	4	5	6	7	8	9	10	11	12	13	14	15	16	WIN or LOSS
7 2/5																W
6 1/5	7 3/4															L
5 2/3	6 2/4	2	5 2/3													W
7 3/4																W
9 4/5	9 3/6															W
5 3/4	3 4/1	11	5/6	9 4/5	5 2/3											W
8 2/6	5 4/4	7 4/4														L
5 4/3	3 4/1	10 5/6	2	4 4/3	6 3/5	6	5 5/5	5 1/4								W
9 2/6	5 2/3	10 4/6	3	8 4/6	8 3/5	6	10 4/6	7 3/4								L
7 4/6																W
10 4/6	4 2/2	8 2/4	7 1/4													L
4 3/5	5 2/3	7 3/4														L
6 4/4	4 3/3	7 2/5														L
11 5/6																W
3 1/4																L
9 4/6	8 4/6	9 4/5														W
8 3/6	8 2/6															W
7 3/4																W
10 4/6	10 4/6															W
8 2/6	9 4/6	2	5 2/3	6 2/4	7 1/4											L
4 3/5	6 2/4	8 3/5	5 1/4	8 3/5	7 3/4											L
7 3/4																W
6 2/4	7 1/6															L
9 4/6	6 3/5	10 4/6	6 3/4	4 3/8	8 3/5	9 4/5										W
9 4/6	7 1/6															L
8 2/3	5 2/3	11	5 5/6	7 1/6												L
7 3/4																W
3 1/4																L
6 2/4	8 3/5	6 2/3														W
6 3/4	8 2/6	8 3/5	8	5 4/4	8 3/5	10 4/6	12 6/6	4 3/3	9 1/6	8 3/5	7 3/4					L
12 6/6																L
6 3/4	4 4/5	6 2/4														W
5 4/4	9 4/6	8 4/3	3 1/4	12 6/4	3	8 4/6	7 2/3									L
9 4/5	5 4/4	9 4/4														W
8 3/4	7 3/4															L
10 4/6	10 4/6															W

Amount Bet									
Pass	Don't Pass	Come	Don't Come	Odds	4 or 10	5 or 9	6 or 8	Result	Total

COMING OUT	2	3	4	5	6	7	8	9	10	11	12	13	14	15	16	WIN or LOSS
10	8	4	5	10												W
10	5	8	4	6	5	6	3	3	5	8	4	7					L
2																L
9	7															L
4	5	8	10	8	10	8	6	3	9	9	7						L
11																W
7																W
9	11	6	7													L
9	10	7														L
7																W
6	6															W
6	6															W
4	6	10	9	3	11	11	9	7								L
3																L
5	6	3	9	6	8	10	5									W
8	3	6	12	10	4	7										L
9	6	6	9													W
9	7															L
10	7															L
5	10	6	5													W
9	11	5	6	4	6	4	7									L
7																W
7																W
8	7															L
11																W
11																W
8	8															W
9	7															L
4	11	7														L
10	9	6	7													L
12																L
10	8	8	5	6	11	8	7									L
10	7															L
6	5	6														W
6	6															W
2																L

				Amount Bet					
Pass	Don't Pass	Come	Don't Come	Odds	4 or 10	5 or 9	6 or 8	Result	Total

COMING OUT	1	2	3	4	5	6	7	8	9	10	11	12	13	14	15	16	WIN or LOSS
10	8	10															W
8	8																W
2																	L
6	4	7															L
10	9	6	3	9	3	8	4	4	11	9	7						L
6	10	9	9	7													L
3																	L
12																	L
8	9	7															L
8	3	10	7														L
7																	W
4	5	8	8	5	10	8	11	6	8	5	3	9	5	6	8		L
11												6	5	9	7		W
9	5	5	4	11	8	6	9										W
4	5	8	6	7													L
10	4	8	8	8	10												W
5	11	6	2	8	9	6	12	7									L
3																	L
8	8																W
3																	L
9	6	4	7														L
5	8	7															L
3																	L
6	10	5	2	4	8	5	5	5	6								W
6	6																W
7																	W
7																	W
8	7																L
6	9	6															W
7																	W
8	6	8															W
7																	W
6	7																L
11																	W
7																	W
10	8	7															L

108

Amount Bet									
Pass	Don't Pass	Come	Don't Come	Odds	4 or 10	5 or 9	6 or 8	Result	Total

COMING OUT	2	3	4	5	6	7	8	9	10	11	12	13	14	15	16	WIN or LOSS
5	10	8	8	9	9	10	6	4	2	7						L
9	6	5	7													L
6	9	9	8	7												L
7																W
6	7															L
8	8															W
11																W
4	8	9	3	5	4											W
7																W
10	10															W
9	11	7														L
3																L
9	7															L
12																L
4	11	4	4													W
4	4															W
3																L
8	5	3	4	9	7											L
7																W
7																W
9	4	7														L
4	4															W
8	5	6	8													W
6	6															W
5	7															L
9	6	9														W
4	11	5	9	2	7											L
8	7															L

Amount Bet									
Pass	Don't Pass	Come	Don't Come	Odds	4 or 10	5 or 9	6 or 8	Result	Total

COMING OUT	2	3	4	5	6	7	8	9	10	11	12	13	14	15	16	WIN or LOSS
6	3	6														W
12																L
8	4	5	5	12	6	7										L
5	8	9	7													L
7																W
8	6	9	5	5	8											W
5	3	8	2	11	7											L
10	8	8	7													L
5	11	6	7													L
9	7															L
4	6	12	6	5	7											L
8	11	6	5	5	4	7										L
9	9															W
11																W
4	11	5	5	8	7											L
7																W
7																W
8	6	3	5	3	6	7										L
9	8	10	2	8	6	7										L
7																W
4	6	8	9	9	6	10	9	12	8	6	4					W
11																W
8	6	7														L
9	6	4	6	10	4	7										L
7																W
7																W
10	5	9	6	9	4	8	7									L
9	8	3	5	7												L
7																W
7																W
9	9															W
6	11	5	7													L
7																W
6	6															W
8	9	4	5	5	9	8										W
6	9	5	5	10	6											W

| Amount Bet | | | | | | | | | |
Pass	Don't Pass	Come	Don't Come	Odds	4 or 10	5 or 9	6 or 8	Result	Total

SANDS: 10/18/78 — 11:45AM – 10:00PM

COMING OUT	1	2	3	4	5	6	7	8	9	10	11	12	13	14	15	16	WIN or LOSS
8	6	12	9	7													L
3																	L
7																	W
4	10	6	6	6	11	5	7										L
8	8																W
8	9	4	11	5	8												W
9	11	8	6	6	11	5	7										L
4	7																L
5	10	5	5														W
6	11	8	8	8	10	6	6										W
5	7																L
6	6																W
5	5																W
5	7																L
4	5	11	11	5	11	8	8	8	5	5	4	4					W
5	7																L
10	9	9	9	7													L
6	11	6															W
5	3	7															L
8	5	7															L
8	9	7															L
8	3	7															L
7																	W
5	11	5															W
7																	W
8	10	10	5	6	8												W
10	6	10															W
4	11	8	7														L
7																	W
5	9	10	4	3	5												W
9	6	12	3	6	6	7											L
7																	W
4	9	10	7														L
2																	L
4	5	6	6	5	8	5	7										L
5	6	9	7														L

114

Amount Bet									
Pass	Don't Pass	Come	Don't Come	Odds	4 or 10	5 or 9	6 or 8	Result	Total

COMING OUT	2	3	4	5	6	7	8	9	10	11	12	13	14	15	16	WIN or LOSS
7																W
5	10	4	5													W
6	8	7														L
7																W
6	7															L
11																W
3																L
6	6															W
6	5	6														W
10	6	8	8	7												L
5	8	9	7													L
10	11	7														L
8	5	9	6	11	6	5	8									W
6	3	6														W
10	4	8	10													W
9	8	8	6	9												W
7																W
3																L
4	5	5	7													L
5	5															W
12																L
7																W
9	5	9														W
5	4	6	4	9	4	4	10	7								L
5	7															L
6	5	6														W
10	9	3	5	6	9	6	7									L
9	9															W
7																W
7																W
6	10	9	3	7												L
11																W
3																L
3																L
7																W
4	6	11	8	8	8	8	6	8	10	6	5	9	5	4		W

Amount Bet									
Pass	Don't Pass	Come	Don't Come	Odds	4 or 10	5 or 9	6 or 8	Result	Total

COMING OUT 1	2	3	4	5	6	7	8	9	10	11	12	13	14	15	16	WIN or LOSS
7																W
5	6	2	2	2	3	8	7									L
7																W
3																L
4	8	8	10	3	9	8	8	5	4							W
7																W
10	4	11	7	7												L
2																L
5	12	5														W
2																L
9	12	6	6	9												W
8	7															L
4	3	10	6	10	9	5	9	6	4							W
6	6															W
4	8	4														W
10	8	8	9	9	9	6	9	8	5	4	12	5	7			L
7																W
8	5	6	3	3	7											L
10	11	8	9	4	7											L
10	7															L
7																W
8	5	7														L
9	9															W
6	5	9	10	3	8	7										L
6	6															W
10	5	5	8	12	10											W
9	5	8	4	10	5	4	11	4	10	10	9					W
2																L
8	8															W
6	6															W
10	5	6	9	12	3	8	6	10								W
4	8	5	5	8	4											W
8	7															L
6	4	5	7													L
5	10	9	5													W
2																L

118

Amount Bet									
Pass	Don't Pass	Come	Don't Come	Odds	4 or 10	5 or 9	6 or 8	Result	Total

COMING OUT	1	2	3	4	5	6	7	8	9	10	11	12	13	14	15	16	WIN or LOSS
11																	W
7																	W
6	6																W
3																	L
6	5	2	10	12	9	7											L
2																	L
7																	W
6	9	7															L
7																	W
4	7																L
8	7																L
3																	L
10	4	9	8	7													L
4	12	6	5	9	7												L
6	12	12	8	6													W
8	9	10	7														L
4	10	7															L
2																	L
6	7																L
5	5																W
12																	L
4	10	10	8	8	3	10	7										L
9	4	8	6	10	7												L
4	9	7															L
9	6	7															L
7																	W
9	9																W
5	9	8	9	8	9	10	4	11	8	7							L
8	5	10	7														L
6	6																W
11																	W
4	8	5	11	8	4												W
10	4	7															L
10	3	10															W
5	10	6	8	6	11	9	2	7									L
8	11	7															L

120

Amount Bet									
Pass	Don't Pass	Come	Don't Come	Odds	4 or 10	5 or 9	6 or 8	Result	Total

SANDS: 10/18/78 — 11:45AM – 10:00PM

COMING OUT	1	2	3	4	5	6	7	8	9	10	11	12	13	14	15	16	WIN or LOSS
10	8	6	7														L
6	8	7															L
7																	W
5	8	5															W
10	4	7															L
11																	W
4	7																L
8	8																W
6	8	6															W
8	5	5	2	5	8												W
7																	W
6	8	5	5	10	7												L
4	5	7															L
7																	W
8	4	5	7														L
10	3	6	7														L
9	5	4	7														L
6	7																L
6	9	6															W
11																	W
4	7																L
8	7																L
5	6	6	5														W
7																	W
6	6																W
12																	L
10	10																W
7																	W
5	9	10	6	6	6	10	5										W
9	7																L
8	11	9	7														L
5	4	12	8	7													L
8	6	3	12	11	4	3	7										L
8	4	2	11	10	11	5	5	7									L
6	8	11	2	6													W
5	7																L

Amount Bet									
Pass	Don't Pass	Come	Don't Come	Odds	4 or 10	5 or 9	6 or 8	Result	Total

COMING OUT	1	2	3	4	5	6	7	8	9	10	11	12	13	14	15	16	WIN or LOSS
7																	W
6	5	5	8	9	7	7											L
3																	L
5	3	6	4	6	6	11	8	7									L
9	3	8	9														W
5	10	5															W
9	9																W
11																	W
10	10																W
9	7																L
4	7																L
5	8	7															L
9	9																W
7																	W
6	7																L
7																	W
6	7																L
10	5	5	6	5	5	8	2	9	9	6	4	8	8	7			L
5	9	7															L
9	3	7															L
4	7																L
9	8	6	9														W
4	8	8	2	8	9	7											L
7																	W
4	5	9	10	2	6	2	12	10	9	7							L
8	4	10	11	8													W
7																	W
5	8	6	5														W
8	5	5	4	11	7												L
8	10	10	8														W
9	8	7															L
5	4	9	3	4	6	6	5										W
6	6																W
6	7																L
6	5	3	6														W
6	4	10	7														L

					Amount Bet				
Pass	Don't Pass	Come	Don't Come	Odds	4 or 10	5 or 9	6 or 8	Result	Total

COMING OUT 1	2	3	4	5	6	7	8	9	10	11	12	13	14	15	16	WIN or LOSS
3																L
3																L
5	11	8	6	3	11	7										L
6	8	8	9	4	5	3	6									W
5	7															L
3																L
7																W
6	6															W
11																W
3																L
9	5	8	7													L
9	7															L
6	8	8	6													W
8	6	7														L
6	5	6														W
6	6															W
7																W
7																W
10	11	5	7													L
7																W
12																L
10	7															L
5	9	8	8	6	7											L
12																L
7																W
7																W
12																L
10	10															W
4	5	8	9	4												W
8	7															L
4	8	9	7													L
4	8	4														W
7																W
7																W
3																L
7																W

Amount Bet									
Pass	Don't Pass	Come	Don't Come	Odds	4 or 10	5 or 9	6 or 8	Result	Total

SANDS: 10/18/78 — 11:45AM – 10:00PM

COMING OUT 1	2	3	4	5	6	7	8	9	10	11	12	13	14	15	16	WIN or LOSS
7¾																W
5¼	5²															W
9⁴	7³															L
4¹	4³															W
6²	8⁵	7¾														L
5²	7⁶															L
10⁵	10⁴															W
11⁵																W
7⁴																W
10⁴	8²	8⁴	3	4	7²											L
6²	9⁵	6²														W
11⁵																W
5¹	6³	8⁵	5²													W
10⁵	8⁵	10⁵														W
10⁵	3¹	8⁴	11	11⁵	9⁴	4	12⁴	9⁴	4³	8³	9⁵	8⁵	7²			L
4¹	7⁵															L
8²	7⁵															L
4¹	9⁴	3	9⁴	10⁵	5⁴	6²	7¹									L
8²	4⁵	10⁵	4³	7¼												L
4¹	8²	5²	9⁵	6³	8⁴	4¹										W
4¹	8²	8²	6²	7¹												L
7¼																W
7⁵																W
9⁵	7²															L
4¹	11⁵	10⁴	7⁴													L
5⁴	8⁵	10⁴	4¹	5²												W
8²	8⁴															W
8²	11	5⁴	8⁴													W
8⁴	3¹	2	7⁵													L
11⁵																W
8²	2¹	10⁵	7³													L
9³	3¹	5¹	9³													W
2¹																L
6²	5⁴	3	7²													L
5²	2¹	6⁵	5²													W
3¹																L

128

					4 or 10	5 or 9	6 or 8		
		Amount Bet							
Pass	Don't Pass	Come	Don't Come	Odds				Result	Total

COMING OUT 1	2	3	4	5	6	7	8	9	10	11	12	13	14	15	16	WIN or LOSS
7																W
3																L
8	10	12	9	4	11	10	8									W
7																W
7																W
10	7															L
4	3	7														L
3																L
6	3	9	8	10	6											W
8	6	7														L
9	7															L
5	8	8	5													W
11																W
7																W
9	9															W
9	5	7														L
9	7															L
2																L
6	7															L
11																W
4	7															L
7																W
7																W
7																W
7																W
3																L
9	3	5	8	8	3	8	5	7								L
5	5															W
9	7															L
6	8	5	8	7												L
9	6	4	4	6	12	7										L
5	5															W
7																W
2																L
9	8	6	8	9												W
4	5	6	6	10	3	5	5	2	5	8	10	11	5	3	5	L
													9	7		

					4 or 10	5 or 9	6 or 8		
			Amount Bet						
Pass	Don't Pass	Come	Don't Come	Odds				Result	Total

COMING OUT 1	2	3	4	5	6	7	8	9	10	11	12	13	14	15	16	WIN or LOSS
5	10	3	8	6	11	6	3	5								W
3																L
8	11	3	9	8	8											W
5	8	5														W
7																W
8	7															L
10	8	4	8	7												L
10	8	6	11	9	4	10										W
11																W
3																L
6	5	8	9	3	6											W
5	7															L
10	8	9	7													L
4	7															L
7																W
7																W
6	6															W
6	11	6														W
8	6	9	9	7												L
3																L
4	5	12	3	12	8	10	8	6	5	6	5	5	5	5	6	L
6	5	6													7	W
9	4	5	8	6	9											W
4	2	9	8	5	10	5	4									W
7																W
9	4	5	8	9	9											W
7																W
6	8	6														W
7																W
6	7															L
10	8	7														L
8	8															W
6	5	8	9	10	4	3	6									W
5	5															W
6	4	12	2	7												L
6	11	11	5	10	5	7										L

	Amount Bet								
Pass	Don't Pass	Come	Don't Come	Odds	4 or 10	5 or 9	6 or 8	Result	Total

SANDS: 10/18/78 – 11:45AM – 10:00PM

1 COMING OUT	2	3	4	5	6	7	8	9	10	11	12	13	14	15	16	WIN or LOSS
6 2/4	11 5/6	10 4/6	6 3/3													W
8 4/4	5 2/3	4 1/3	6 2/4	7 2/5												L
9 3/6	6 2/4	5 2/3	7 1/6													L
9 4/5	10 4/6	7 2/5														L
7 1/6																W
8 4/4	7 2/5															L
8 2/6	9 4/5	9 3/6	3 1/2	5 1/4	8 2/6											W
4 1/3	6 1/5	9 3/6	5 1/4	9 4/5	7 3/4											L
3 1/2																L
9 4/5	10 4/6	6 2/4	7 2/5													L
7 1/6																W
2 1/1																L
3 1/2																L
10 4/6	3 1/2	11 5/6	7 3/4													L
9 3/6	2 1/1	8 2/6	8 2/6	7 2/5												L
6 1/5	8 2/6	7 1/6														L
7 1/6																W
7 3/4																W
10 4/6	7 2/5															L
3 1/2																L
8 2/6	12 6/6	7 2/5														L
8 2/6	7 3/4															L
4 1/3	11 5/6	4 1/3														W
6 3/3	4 1/3	10 5/5	9 4/5	6 1/5												W
4 2/2	9 3/6	7 3/4														L
11 5/6																W
7 1/6																W
8 3/5	8 2/6															W
9 3/6	4 1/3	6 1/5	6 1/5	7 1/6												L
2 1/1																L
6 3/3	9 3/6	2 1/1	2 1/1	5 2/3	6 2/4											W
6 1/5	4 2/2	10 5/5	6 2/4													W
7 3/4																W
7 2/5																W
2 1/1																L
6 2/4	4 2/2	7 3/4														L

	Amount Bet								
Pass	Don't Pass	Come	Don't Come	Odds	4 or 10	5 or 9	6 or 8	Result	Total

SANDS: 10/18/78 — 11:45AM – 10:00PM

COMING OUT (1)	2	3	4	5	6	7	8	9	10	11	12	13	14	15	16	WIN or LOSS
4	9	4														W
10	10															W
3																L
6	7															L
8	7															L
9	11	7														L
7																W
6	6															W
3																L
10	4	5	7													L
8	6	7														L
9	5	9														W
8	5	7														L
5	7															L
3																L
4	8	7														L
6	5	11	7													L
8	6	7														L

Amount Bet									
Pass	Don't Pass	Come	Don't Come	Odds	4 or 10	5 or 9	6 or 8	Result	Total

COMING OUT 1	2	3	4	5	6	7	8	9	10	11	12	13	14	15	16	WIN or LOSS
9	9															W
11																W
9	4	12	9													W
5	9	6	3	6	10	6	10	5								W
3																L
9	7															L
8	6	4	9	12	6	3	7									L
8	9	7														L
6	5	9	8	7												L
11																W
4	7															L
7																W
12																L
8	3	10	7													L
7																W
5	9	7														L
5	6	7														L
4	3	6	5	6	10	8	8	6	9	8	4					W
12																L
9	12	7														L
6	12	6														W
7																W
7																W
10	6	10														W
10	5	8	4	2	6	7										L
3																L
7																W
5	6	7														L
7																W
6	5	7														L
10	8	6	5	7												L
4	12	9	7													L
5	10	10	7													L
9	6	6	11	3	9											W
8	3	9	5	9	12	3	5	4	10	11	3	8				W
6	6															W

138

Amount Bet									
Pass	Don't Pass	Come	Don't Come	Odds	4 or 10	5 or 9	6 or 8	Result	Total

COMING OUT 1	2	3	4	5	6	7	8	9	10	11	12	13	14	15	16	WIN or LOSS
7																W
5	5															W
5	4	3	5													W
10	6	3	4	10												W
9	4	6	6	8	10	10	6	8	8	3	6	5	8	9		W
8	5	6	11	11	4	7										L
7																W
11																W
7																W
3																L
6	7															L
6	10	4	7													L
10	4	4	2	6	4	6	6	9	7							L
10	5	6	7													L
11																W
8	7															L
7																W
2																L
6	11	10	9	8	12	9	11	8	4	6						W
5	8	9	10	4	7											L
9	10	6	9													W
8	5	9	11	4	5	6	8									W
4	8	9	5	4												W
10	10															W
9	11	5	10	11	10	9										W
4	9	2	6	5	7											L
11																W
4	7															L
5	5															W
11																W
3																L
6	4	5	8	7												L
12																L
7																W
3																L
10	9	2	9	4	8	8	7									L

Amount Bet									
Pass	Don't Pass	Come	Don't Come	Odds	4 or 10	5 or 9	6 or 8	Result	Total

NUGGET: 10/19/78 — 12:15PM – 10:15PM

1 COMING OUT	2	3	4	5	6	7	8	9	10	11	12	13	14	15	16	WIN or LOSS
5 2/3	6 1/5	5 2/3														W
7 3/4																W
11 5/6																W
5 1/4	10 5/5	7 2/5														L
8 3/5	6 1/5	6 2/4	7 1/6													L
3 1/2																L
5 1/4	6 2/4	4 1/3	9 3/6	5 2/3												W
4 1/3	5 1/4	5 2/3	9 4/5	10 4/6	5 2/3	11 5/6	5 1/4	5 2/3	3 1/2	7 3/4						L
11 5/6																W
4 1/3	4 1/3															W
7 1/6																W
9 4/5	9 4/5															W
6 1/5	8 4/4	3 1/2	8 2/6	8 2/6	10 4/6	2 1/1	7 3/4									L
8 2/6	9 4/5	8 2/6														W
7 3/4																W
7 1/6																W
7 1/6																W
2 1/1																L
4 1/3	9 4/5	7 3/4														L
5 2/3	6 1/5	7 3/4														L
8 2/6	7 2/5															L
5 2/3	3 1/2	7 3/4														L
4 1/3	8 2/6	5 1/4	3 1/2	12 6/6	5 1/4	3 1/2	5 2/3	9 4/5	7 2/5							L
6 1/5	4 2/2	9 4/5	5 1/4	4 2/2	3 1/2	5 1/4	5 2/3	10 4/6	7 3/4							L
9 3/6	8 2/6	8 2/6	10 4/6	6 3/3	8 3/5	3 1/2	10 4/6	10 4/6	3 1/2	5 1/4	5 1/4	8 3/5	6 1/5	7 3/4		L
12 6/6																L
7 1/6																W
7 1/6																W
5 2/3	12 6/6	9 4/5	9 3/6	7 1/6												L
8 3/5	8 3/5															W
6 1/5	5 1/4	11 5/6	7 3/4													L
6 3/3	10 4/6	10 4/6	3 1/2	6 1/5												W
9 3/6	3 1/2	8 4/4	5 2/3	9 3/6												W
3 1/2																L
7 1/6																W
7 3/4																W

Amount Bet									
Pass	Don't Pass	Come	Don't Come	Odds	4 or 10	5 or 9	6 or 8	Result	Total

NUGGET: 10/19/78 — 12:15PM – 10:15PM

COMING OUT 1	2	3	4	5	6	7	8	9	10	11	12	13	14	15	16	WIN or LOSS
4 1/3	5 1/4	5 2/3	11 5/6	9 4/5	3 1/2	7 3/4										L
3 1/2																L
5 2/3	6 1/5	12 6/6	8 2/6	11 5/6	4 2/2	6 2/4	4 2/2	9 3/6	3 1/2	11 5/6	8 3/5	10 4/6	5 2/3			W
7 2/5																W
8 3/5	3 1/2	7 2/5														L
8 3/5	7 3/4															L
9 3/6	6 2/4	7 3/4														L
9 3/6	7 1/6															L
11 5/6																W
9 4/5	10 4/6	8 3/5	9 3/6													W
9 4/5	11 5/6	7 3/4														L
9 3/6	6 2/4	11 5/6	4 1/3	5 2/3	5 1/4	9 4/5										W
7 2/5																W
7 2/5																W
6 1/5	9 4/5	10 4/6	9 3/6	5 2/3	4 1/3	6 1/5										W
7 2/5																W
4 1/3	5 1/4	12 6/6	5 2/3	8 3/5	5 1/4	3 1/2	8 3/5	9 4/5	7 1/6							L
6 1/5	7 2/5															L
8 4/4	9 3/6	6 1/5	5 2/3	8 2/6												W
5 1/4	9 3/6	7 3/4														L
7 3/4																W
7 1/6																W
10 4/6	9 4/5	5 2/3	4 1/3	5 1/4	7 3/4											L
7 3/4																W
7 3/4																W
6 2/4	9 4/5	8 2/6	6 2/4													W
10 4/6	6 1/5	4 1/3	9 3/6	5 1/4	6 3/3	2 1/1	6 2/4	6 1/5	7 2/5							L
9 3/6	5 2/3	8 2/6	8 2/6	8 3/5	12 6/6	9 4/5										W
10 5/5	8 3/5	6 3/3	9 3/6	10 4/6												W
9 3/6	10 4/6	6 1/5	6 3/3	6 2/4	10 5/5	8 3/5	6 2/4	3 1/2	2 1/1	7 1/6						L
8 3/5	11 5/6	5 1/4	10 4/6	8 3/5												W
6 1/5	8 3/5	8 2/6	5 1/4	6 2/4												W
10 5/5	7 2/5															L
6 1/5	7 2/5															L
9 4/5	7 3/4															L
7 3/4																W

Amount Bet									
Pass	Don't Pass	Come	Don't Come	Odds	4 or 10	5 or 9	6 or 8	Result	Total

COMING OUT	2	3	4	5	6	7	8	9	10	11	12	13	14	15	16	WIN or LOSS
4	10	9	5	5	5	6	8	4	4							W
8	4	8														W
7																W
6	8	10	7													L
10	9	8	4	12	4	5	9	5	6	8	3	7				L
4	9	12	3	10	5	11	3	8	8	5	12	7				L
7																W
4	7															L
6	4	5	5	7												L
5	5															W
6	6															W
6	3	4	6													W
7																W
10	7															L
9	6	7														L
6	7															L
5	5															W
5	9	10	7													L
6	7															L
5	2	4	9	12	7											L
6	5	6														W
6	7															L
3																L
5	10	6	9	9	3	5										W
9	7															L
11																W
12																L
10	7															L
7																W
4	5	8	11	4												W
7																W
8	8															W
3																L
8	5	10	7													L
7																W
6	6															W

146

Amount Bet									
Pass	Don't Pass	Come	Don't Come	Odds	4 or 10	5 or 9	6 or 8	Result	Total

NUGGET: 10/19/78 — 12:15PM — 10:15PM

COMING OUT 1	2	3	4	5	6	7	8	9	10	11	12	13	14	15	16	WIN or LOSS
6	6															W
5	9	11	10	4	9	4	12	10	9	8	5	5				W
5	12	12	11	4	7											L
11																W
9	11	5	10	7												L
9	3	10	5	9												W
4	10	8	7													L
7																W
7																W
6	7															L
7																W
7																W
6	3	10	8	8	11	5	8	6								W
5	11	9	8	5												W
6	7															L
7																W
9	12	8	7													L
9	7															L
6	7															L
6	7															L
5	8	9	9	10	8	7										L
8	5	7														L
8	3	6	5	6	6	7										L
7																W
7																W
9	6	8	11	9												W
9	6	9														W
9	12	3	4	6	9											W
10	9	6	9	10												W
3																L
3																L
7																W
5	8	9	2	2	11	10	7									L
3																L
6	5	4	8	8	7											L
4	5	8	6	5	6	4										W

Amount Bet									
Pass	Don't Pass	Come	Don't Come	Odds	4 or 10	5 or 9	6 or 8	Result	Total

NUGGET: 10/19/78 — 12:15PM – 10:15PM

COMING OUT	1	2	3	4	5	6	7	8	9	10	11	12	13	14	15	16	WIN or LOSS
6	10	11	7														L
3																	L
3																	L
6	10	6															W
8	4	4	10	8													W
7																	W
6	9	10	7														L
11																	W
4	2	11	7														L
7																	W
9	5	7															L
9	11	5	8	10	10	5	5	7									L
3																	L
7																	W
11																	W
9	8	7															L
6	7																L
9	8	7															L
9	4	5	10	8	8	8	11	10	3	9							W
8	3	7															L
6	9	5	9	6													W
6	8	4	3	7													L
8	2	6	2	6	9	11	5	8									W
8	8																W
3																	L
4	9	7															L
7																	W
8	3	11	7														L
4	8	11	4														W
7																	W
4	8	4															W
7																	W
6	5	8	7														L
12																	L
3																	L
6	3	9	5	11	10	5	7										L

GAMBLER'S BOOK CLUB THOMAS MIDGLEY

					Amount Bet				
Pass	Don't Pass	Come	Don't Come	Odds	4 or 10	5 or 9	6 or 8	Result	Total

COMING OUT	2	3	4	5	6	7	8	9	10	11	12	13	14	15	16	WIN or LOSS
8²⁄₆	3	¹⁄₂12	⁶⁄₆4	⁴⁄₃11	⁵⁄₆7	²⁄₅										L
5⁴⁄₅	7	³⁄₄														L
7²⁄₅																W
8²⁄₆	5	⁴⁄₄7	²⁄₆													L
2⁴⁄																L
6³⁄₆	4	²⁄₆7	³⁄₄													L
4⁵⁄10	⁴⁄₆8	²⁄₆5	⁴⁄₃7	²⁄₅												L
9²⁄₆7	³⁄₄															L
5⁴⁄8	⁴⁄₆8	³⁄10	⁴⁄₆3	⁴⁄8	⁴⁄9	⁴⁄9	⁴⁄11	⁵⁄7	³⁄₄							L
8⁶⁄6	⁴⁄₃4	³⁄11	⁵⁄6	⁴⁄7	²⁄₄											L
6⁵⁄10	⁵⁄₆7	⁴⁄₆														L
7⁴⁄₆																W
5²⁄₆7	³⁄₄															L
11																W
5²⁄₆7	³⁄₅															L
10⁶⁄9	³⁄₆6	⁴⁄₆6	²⁄₇8	²⁄₄4	⁴⁄3	⁶⁄₃5	⁴⁄4	⁴⁄5	⁴⁄9	²⁄₆6	⁵⁄7	³⁄₄				L
6⁴⁄10	⁴⁄₆5	⁵⁄8	⁵⁄₆6	²⁄₄												W
5⁴⁄4	⁴⁄₄7	²⁄₅														L
4²⁄₆6	⁴⁄₆6	³⁄8	⁵⁄₆6	⁴⁄7	²⁄₅											L
8⁴⁄8	²⁄₆															W
3⁴⁄																L
8³⁄₆8	²⁄₆															W
10⁴⁄₆4	⁵⁄3	⁴⁄₄11	⁵⁄₆4	⁴⁄₃10	⁵⁄₆											W
7⁴⁄₆																W
7⁴⁄₆																W
7⁴⁄₆																W
7⁴⁄₆																W
4⁴⁄4	⁴⁄₆															W
8⁵⁄₂2	⁴⁄7	⁴⁄₂4	²⁄₂9	³⁄₆4	³⁄8	⁴⁄₅										W
9³⁄₂3	⁴⁄₄4	⁴⁄₆6	⁴⁄7	⁴⁄₆												L
10⁵⁄10	⁴⁄₆															W
9⁴⁄5	²⁄₃8	³⁄₆7	³⁄₄													L
9³⁄11	⁵⁄₆9	⁴⁄₄														W
7²⁄₅																W
7³⁄₅																W
4⁴⁄11	⁵⁄₆10	⁴⁄₆7	²⁄₅													L

Amount Bet									
Pass	Don't Pass	Come	Don't Come	Odds	4 or 10	5 or 9	6 or 8	Result	Total

COMING OUT 1	2	3	4	5	6	7	8	9	10	11	12	13	14	15	16	WIN or LOSS
7																W
6	9	9	7													L
6	3	12	8	10	9	12	3	2	8	9	7					L
6	10	5	2	3	8	7										L
12																L
7																W
8	10	9	6	6	6	7										L
2																L
2																L
6	7															L
7																W
4	6	7														L
6	4	7														L
3																L
6	6															W
8	3	10	6	10	10	8	8									W
9	11	5	7													L
4	9	7														L
8	9	5	7													L
4	7															L
6	9	7														L
5	10	11	4	8	8	7										L
10	7															L
9	4	7														L
10	11	7														L
11																W
6	7															L
5	8	8	8	9	6	5										W
8	8															W
10	6	10														W
7																W
10	9	6	3	11	6	6	6	8	8	10						W
12																L
4	6	9	8	8	7											L
8	2	7														L
9	5	7														L

154

Amount Bet									
Pass	Don't Pass	Come	Don't Come	Odds	4 or 10	5 or 9	6 or 8	Result	Total

COMING OUT	2	3	4	5	6	7	8	9	10	11	12	13	14	15	16	WIN or LOSS
10	9	6	5	7												L
4	7															L
9	4	6	8	6	4	4	4	3	7							L
8	9	6	9	10	7											L
9	5	10	5	4	7											L
10	7															L
6	5	4	10	8	7											L
5	2	5														W
6	8	3	7													L
5	6	8	10	7												L
8	10	12	9	9	9	8										W
6	8	9	8	6												W
6	5	4	3	7												L
7																W
10	9	7														L
3																L
4	7															L
6	3	4	8	5	9	4	6									W
9	6	5	9													W
8	12	9	6	11	6	7										L
7																W
10	11	3	10													W
10	12	10														W
11																W
10	10															W
5	5															W
5	6	7														L
8	7															L
6	5	7														L
11																W
4	9	7														L
9	10	3	9													W
9	5	6	6	10	11	4	9									W
7																W
7																W
6	4	12	8	6												W

					Amount Bet				
Pass	Don't Pass	Come	Don't Come	Odds	4 or 10	5 or 9	6 or 8	Result	Total

COMING OUT	1	2	3	4	5	6	7	8	9	10	11	12	13	14	15	16	WIN or LOSS
11																	W
8	8																W
12																	L
8	9	8															W
8	5	9	9	10	9	7	7										L
7																	W
5	9	9	10	7													L
5	6	6	6	3	6	3	7										L
8	7																L
2																	L
9	7																L
6	8	7															L
12																	L
8	7																L
11																	W
7																	W
5	2	6	11	11	5	5											W
11																	W
9	8	7															L
5	10	11	7														L
2																	L
10	9	7															L
6	11	5	3	5	8	12	5	5	9	5	11	10	2	2	5		W
5	6	3	8	9	8	9	8	3	6	4	5				6		W
12																	L
7																	W
10	5	10															W
11																	W
5	7																L
4	6	9	7														L
5	8	6	10	3	5												W
7																	W
8	10	5	12	9	6	5	6	4	4	5	2	11	5	6	6		W
9	8	11	4	3	7							10	11	8			L
4	5	4															W
10	9	7															L

158

Amount Bet									
Pass	Don't Pass	Come	Don't Come	Odds	4 or 10	5 or 9	6 or 8	Result	Total

COMING OUT	2	3	4	5	6	7	8	9	10	11	12	13	14	15	16	WIN or LOSS
6	2	5	10	9	5	5	7									L
7																W
10	7															L
5	9	10	8	8	5											W
6	7															L
11																W
8	5	7														L
8	8															W
4	6	10	8	10	10	6	6	7								L
11																W
4	11	7														L
5	9	6	9	9	6	5										W
5	7															L
3																L
5	11	10	7													L
4	10	3	6	4												W
2																L
10	9	8	10													W
7																W
9	6	11	4	4	10	3	4	7								L
7																W
7																W
7																W
11																W
5	9	10	6	11	5	7										L
4	11	10	10	6	5	6	8	4								W
7																W
6	4	4	6													W
11																W
9	6	5	9													W
9	5	11	8	8	9											W
8	8															W
8	4	9	8													W
5	8	6	8	7												L
10	3	4	7													L
3																L

Amount Bet									
Pass	Don't Pass	Come	Don't Come	Odds	4 or 10	5 or 9	6 or 8	Result	Total

COMING OUT	1	2	3	4	5	6	7	8	9	10	11	12	13	14	15	16	WIN or LOSS
4	9	10	8	2	7	7											L
5	3	6	5														W
5	8	8	9	6	7												L
3																	L
8	4	7															L
9	6	4	7														L
7																	W
8	7																L
8	8																W
5	8	5															W
7																	W
7																	W
4	5	5	8	7													L
6	7																L
10	3	9	7														L
8	5	6	9	8													W
4	10	10	8	8	8	4											W
8	8																W
3																	L
8	10	7															L
3																	L
10	11	7															L
4	3	5	6	7													L
3																	L
6	3	8	6														W
10	8	6	6	7													L
7																	W
8	2	6	8														W
3																	L
7																	W
4	8	8	5	7													L
11																	W
7																	W
7																	W
8	9	2	5	4	6	6	9	9	9	7							L
9	8	8	8	9													W

162

Amount Bet									
Pass	Don't Pass	Come	Don't Come	Odds	4 or 10	5 or 9	6 or 8	Result	Total

NUGGET: 10/19/78 — 12:15PM — 10:15PM

COMING OUT	2	3	4	5	6	7	8	9	10	11	12	13	14	15	16	WIN or LOSS
6	8	8	7													L
7																W
3																L
5	6	10	3	2	7											L
10	2	6	11	9	8	8	8	10								W
5	3	4	10	8	5											W
5	4	3	6	7												L
10	7															L
10	4	11	6	3	8	6	8	8	6	9	8	2	9	7		L
7																W
9	4	6	7													L
4	5	9	6	8	6	9	9	10	7							L
10	4	8	6	9	6	9	8	8	6	7						L
3																L
11																W
10	10															W
9	9															W
6	8	7														L
9	10	7														L
6	7															L
10	8	9	11	7												L
6	9	7														L
4	5	6	5	8	6	4										W
11																W
4	9	10	7													L
6	11	4	7													L
12																L
5	9	4	4	11	5											W
6	9	8	6													W
5	9	9	11	4	9	9	8	8	7							L
10	6	7														L
7																W
6	9	7														L
8	8															W
8	3	5	6	5	5	4	4	12	9	9	3	8				W
6	9	11	7													L

164

	Amount Bet								
Pass	Don't Pass	Come	Don't Come	Odds	4 or 10	5 or 9	6 or 8	Result	Total

NUGGET: 10/19/78 — 12:15PM – 10:15PM

COMING OUT	1	2	3	4	5	6	7	8	9	10	11	12	13	14	15	16	WIN or LOSS
10	5	6	10														W
9	6	7															L
11																	W
5	10	4	12	10	9	9	9	6	10	2	10	5					W
5	6	9	9	6	7												L
7																	W
6	7																L
9	5	4	9														W
6	10	3	4	8	8	4	11	10	2	6							W
2																	L
10	6	8	7														L
5	7																L
6	7																L
8	7																L
5	4	5															W
10	9	8	8	12	9	4	5	7									L
4	4																W
4	7																L
10	8	9	4	4	10												W
8	5	4	8														W
9	4	5	2	6	5	9											W
11																	W
8	5	4	5	9	10	9	6	9	7								L
4	7																L
10	10																W
8	7																L
8	11	8															W
6	9	8	4	4	8	9	5	7									L
4	9	6	5	3	8	8	7										L
6	9	5	10	6													W
6	9	11	10	12	8	10	7										L
10	3	7															L
11																	W
2																	L
5	7																L
8	7																L

Pass	Don't Pass	Come	Don't Come	Odds	4 or 10	5 or 9	6 or 8	Result	Total
			Amount Bet						

COMING OUT 1	2	3	4	5	6	7	8	9	10	11	12	13	14	15	16	WIN or LOSS
10 5/6	7 1/2															L
6 1/5	8 4/5	5 2/3	9 2/3	3	4 1/4	4 4/5	8 2/5	8 4/4	9 4/5	12 5/6	9 4/5	6 3/5				W
7 3/4																W
7 1/5																W
11 5/6																W
8 3/5	5 2/3	9 4/5	11	7 1/6												L
7 1/5																W
9 4/5	11 5/6	7 1/6														L
5 1/3	9 4/5	8 2/3	8 1/3	2	6 4/5	12 5/6	8 2/5	7 2/5								L
3 1/4																L
6 1/3	6 1/4															W
11 1/6																W
6 4/5	7 1/2															L
8 4/5	6 1/3	6 1/4	7 3/4													L
12 5/6																L
4 1/3	7 2/5															L
3 1/4																L
11 5/6																W
9 2/5	4 2/3	6 2/5	6 1/3	3 1/2	10 4/5	8 2/5	6 4/5	8 4/4	8 2/5	7 1/6						L
6 3/5	9 4/4	8 2/3	11	6 1/3												W
9 3/5	7 1/6															L
7 2/5																W
8 4/4	12 4/6	8 2/3														W
9 4/5	9 4/4															W
7 1/5																W
4 2/3	7 1/6															L
4 2/3	11 4/5	8 4/4	10 5/5	6 3/5	7 3/4											L
7 1/5																W
7 3/5																W
7 1/5																W
10 4/5	8 2/3	8 2/3	6 3/5	7 3/4												L
7 3/5																W
2 1/5																L
3 1/5																L
3 1/5																L
6 4/5	7 2/6															L

				Amount Bet					
Pass	Don't Pass	Come	Don't Come	Odds	4 or 10	5 or 9	6 or 8	Result	Total

COMING OUT 1	2	3	4	5	6	7	8	9	10	11	12	13	14	15	16	WIN or LOSS
2																L
4	7															L
5	5															W
10	8	9	9	10												W
9	7															L
9	10	4	6	7												L
8	6	4	4	5	8											W
7																W
7																W
5	11	9	7													L
10	3	9	6	7												L
5	11	8	10	9	5											W
10	5	6	4	8	10											W
5	2	3	8	2	4	3	7									L
2																L
8	10	7														L
3																L
6	8	10	5	7												L
6	5	10	5	7												L
6	6															W
9	9															W
5	6	8	6	12	2	5										W
3																L
2																L
6	8	11	8	3	7											L
8	9	10	5	6	11	9	7									L
4	4															W
6	4	7														L
6	5	9	6													W
4	4															W
2																L
5	8	7														L
11																W
2																L
4	11	7														L
6	2	7														L

Amount Bet									
Pass	Don't Pass	Come	Don't Come	Odds	4 or 10	5 or 9	6 or 8	Result	Total

COMING OUT 1	2	3	4	5	6	7	8	9	10	11	12	13	14	15	16	WIN or LOSS
5	7															L
11																W
4	7															L
7																W
10	3	11	6	2	8	2	7									L
8	4	11	12	9	7											L
7																W
2																L
7																W
6	8	8	8	9	11	5	10	9	3	9	5	5	8	6	4	W
9	3	11	7											3	6	L
6	7															L
8	10	8														W
8	6	6	7													L
8	11	4	3	7												L
8	7															L
7																W
8	4	5	7													L
7																W
6	5	7														L
7																W
4	8	7														L
6	3	4	4	9	7											L
8	7															L
3																L
11																W
9	3	9														W
4	10	3	7													L
7																W
8	8															W
4	6	4														W
6	3	7														L
5	8	8	8	2	9	6	9	8	4	9	5					W
5	11	2	7													L
6	7															L
11																W

					Amount Bet				
Pass	Don't Pass	Come	Don't Come	Odds	4 or 10	5 or 9	6 or 8	Result	Total

COMING OUT	1	2	3	4	5	6	7	8	9	10	11	12	13	14	15	16	WIN or LOSS
5	6	6	8	4	7												L
5	11	3	5														W
10	6	11	5	8	6	8	4	2	2	9	7						L
4	5	9	10	7													L
10	2	5	3	9	4	6	9	10									W
9	9																W
6	8	6															W
4	9	6	5	3	8	8	5	9	3	3	8	5	8	7			L
9	6	7															L
4	7																L
9	10	6	6	8	11	8	7										L
11																	W
3																	L
11																	W
4	6	5	3	10	6	6	8	4	4								W
9	5	7															L
8	6	4	6	2	7												L
5	2	6	8	10	3	3	9	7									L
9	6	3	3	4	6	7											L
6	7																L
3																	L
7																	W
7																	W
7																	W
3																	L
5	7																L
6	6																W
3																	L
6	8	4	9	3	7												L
3																	L
8	4	8															W
10	5	6	5	6	7												L
8	5	3	3	6	6	7											L
8	9	9	9	10	5	8											W
11																	W
8	10	9	7														L

Amount Bet									
Pass	Don't Pass	Come	Don't Come	Odds	4 or 10	5 or 9	6 or 8	Result	Total

NUGGET: 10/19/78 – 12:15PM – 10:15PM

1 - COMING OUT	2	3	4	5	6	7	8	9	10	11	12	13	14	15	16	WIN or LOSS
7 2/5																W
8 4/4	8 3/5															W
11 5/6																W
9 4/5	6 2/4	4 2/2	10 4/6	5 1/4	6 1/5	5 1/4	7 3/4									L
12 6/6																L
8 2/6	3 1/2	6 2/4	7 1/6													L
4 1/3	9 4/5	7 2/5														L
2 1/1																L
11 5/6																W
8 2/6	5 2/3	7 1/6														L
7 1/6																W
10 4/6	6 3/3	6 1/5	3 1/2	8 3/5	12 6/6	11 5/6	4 1/3	9 4/5	7 3/4							L
8 3/5	7 3/4															L
6 2/4	10 5/5	11 5/6	8 3/5	4 1/3	9 3/6	7 1/6										L
4 1/3	7 2/5															L
12 6/6																L
7 3/4																W
4 1/3	6 2/4	2 1/1	10 4/6	5 1/4	7 1/6											L
7 3/4																W
7 1/6																W
8 3/5	7 3/4															L
5 1/4	6 3/3	9 4/5	6 3/3	9 4/5	4 1/3	10 4/6	3 1/2	12 6/6	5 1/4							W
7 3/4																W
3 1/2																L
4 1/3	2 1/1	7 1/6														L
8 4/4	4 1/3	6 2/4	4 1/3	5 2/3	10 4/6	8 4/4										W
11 5/6																W
10 4/6	11 5/6	10 4/6														W
8 2/6	6 2/4	11 5/6	10 4/6	6 1/5	9 4/5	7 2/5										L
10 4/6	8 4/4	5 2/3	5 2/3	11 5/6	9 4/5	10 4/6										W
7 1/6																W
5 1/4	9 3/6	10 5/5	6 1/5	5 1/4												W
9 3/6	4 2/2	6 2/4	9 4/5													W
8 2/6	9 3/6	9 3/6	6 2/4	9 3/6	7 3/4											L
7 2/5																W
6 1/5	12 6/6	8 4/4	8 2/6	6 1/5												W

	Amount Bet								
Pass	Don't Pass	Come	Don't Come	Odds	4 or 10	5 or 9	6 or 8	Result	Total

NUGGET: 10/19/78 — 12:15PM – 10:15PM

COMING OUT	1	2	3	4	5	6	7	8	9	10	11	12	13	14	15	16	WIN or LOSS
	9	6	9														W
	7																W
	6	9	12	8	8	8	10	7									L
	10	4	11	6	10												W
	7																W
	5	8	6	10	8	11	10	12	8	8	7						L
	8	3	6	11	7												L
	8	7															L
	6	11	11	9	4	6											W
	7																W
	5	5															W
	7																W
	4	9	6	5	5	6	12	6	6	9	4						W
	6	9	8	7													L
	6	10	6														W
	6	8	3	4	5	9	5	3	7								L
	4	4															W
	8	10	3	4	6	4	8										W
	7																W
	9	3	7														L

Amount Bet									
Pass	Don't Pass	Come	Don't Come	Odds	4 or 10	5 or 9	6 or 8	Result	Total

11 LAST WORD

If you expected this book to instantly make you a millionaire—or if you expected to find the secret to spending a weekend in Las Vegas or Atlantic City and win enough money to instantly retire—you are no doubt disappointed. The purpose of this book is to make you a smarter craps strategy while giving you a more intelligent, insider view of the game.

You will find this to be a great companion to my other book, *Craps: A Smart Shooters Guide*, where I give players a scientific and mathematically proven way to determine what the dice are doing—and how to take advantage of their cycles. Like this book, I rely on the results of the 7,500 dice rolls and the theoretical results a player can expect.

I hope you've learned a lot about the game of craps and can use your newfound knowledge to take the craps table for a good ride!

 **GLOSSARY**

Any Craps:
A bet that the next roll will be a 2, 3, or 12.

Any Seven:
A bet that the next roll will be a 7.

Back Line:
Refers to the don't pass area.

Bar the 12:
A term found in the don't pass and don't come areas which makes the roll of a 12 (in some casinos the 2) a push between the wrong player and the house.

Big 6, and Big 8:
A bet that the 6, or the 8, whichever is bet, will be thrown before a 7 is rolled.

Box Numbers:
The boxes numbered, 4, 5, 6, 8, 9, and 10, which are used to mark the point, and to mark place, come, and buy bets.

Center Bets:
The bets located in the center of the layout.

Cold Dice:
A streak of losing rolls for the right bettors. Good for wrong bettors.

Come Bet:

A bet that the dice will win, or pass. Works just like a pass bet except that it can only be made after a point is established.

Come Bet Coming Out Roll:

When a pass line point is already established, the first roll of the dice after a come bet is placed and before the come point is established.

Come Point:

The throw of a 4, 5, 6, 8, 9, or 10 on the come bet coming-out roll becomes the come point number.

Coming-Out Roll:

The roll made before any point has been established.

Coming Out:

A term to designate that a new come-out roll is about to happen.

Contract Bet:

A bet that, once placed, cannot be removed until a conclusion to it has been reached.

Correct Odds:

The mathematical likelihood that a bet will be a winner, expressed in odds.

Crap Out:

The roll of a 2, 3, or 12 on a coming-out roll, an automatic loser for pass line bettors.

Craps:

Term used to denote a 2, 3, or 12. Also the name of the game.

Craps-Eleven:

A one roll bet combining the Any Craps and 11.

Dealer:

The casino employee who works directly with the player and who handles all monetary transactions and bets.

Dice:

The two six-sided cubes, numbered one to six, that are used to play craps.

Don't Come Bet:

A bet made against the dice. The bet works just like the don't pass except that it can only be made after a point is established.

Don't Pass:

A bet made before a point is established, on the coming-out roll only, that the dice will lose.

Don't Pass Bet Decision:

A don't pass bet that gets completed as either a winning or losing bet.

Double Odds Bet:

A free-odds bet that allows the player to bet double his line wager as a right bettor, and double the line payoff as a wrong bettor.

Down:

An instruction for a dealer to pick up place bets from the numbers and return them to the player.

Easy, Easy Way:

The throw of a 4, 6, 8, or 10 other than as a pair, such as a 1 and a 5, 6, the easy way.

Edge, House Edge:

The built-in odds that favor the casino over the player.

Even-Money:

The payoff of one dollar for every dollar bet.

GLOSSARY

Fade a Bet:

To put up money and cover a bet.

Fading Game:

A private crap game where players, on a rotating basis, shoot the dice and put up money to gamble—and the other players cover the shooter's bets.

Field Bet:

A one-roll bet that the next roll of the dice will be a number in the field box—a 2, 3, 4, 9, 10, 11, or 12.

Field Numbers:

Numbers rolled that would be winners on the field bet—2, 3, 4, 9, 10, 11 and 12.

Floorman:

Casino executive who supervises one or more craps tables.

Free-Odds Bets:

A bet made in conjunction with the line, come, and don't come bets, that can only be made after the establishment of a point or come point. The free-odds bet is paid off at the correct odds, with the house having no advantage.

Front Line:

Refers to the pass line.

Hand:

A sequence of rolls that is completed when the roller throws a 7 after having established a point on a coming out roll.

Hardway Bet:

A sequence bet that the hardway number, the 4, 6, 8, or 10, will come up in doubles before it comes up easy, or before a 7 is thrown.

Hardway:

The throw of a 4, 6, 8 or 10 as a pair, such as 3, 3, 6 the hardway.

Horn Bet:

A one roll bet that the next throw will be a 2, 3, 11, or 12.

Hot Roll:

An extended succession of winning throws for players betting with the dice. Bad for wrong bettors.

House:

A term to denote the casino.

Inside Numbers:

The place numbers 5, 6, 8, and 9.

Insurance:

A bet made to "protect" another bet—the wager wins on the rolls that the main bet loses on.

Lay Bet:

A wager made by wrong bettors that a 7 will show before the point number.

Layout:

The felted surface of the craps table where bets are placed, paid off and collected, and where the dice are thrown.

Lay-up Odds:

The odds wagered in conjunction with a don't pass or don't come bet.

Line Bet:

Refers to a pass or don't pass bet.

Making a Pass:

Throwing a natural on the first roll or making a point.

Odds:

The number of times an event is likely to happen compared to the number of times the event is likely not to happen. For example, out of the 36 possible combinations on a pair of dice, one of them is 2 (1 + 1) making the odds against a single roll of 2 on the dice 35 to 1.

Odds Bet:

See Free-Odds Bet.

Off:

A designation that a bet is not working on a particular roll.

On:

A designation that a bet is working on a particular roll.

Outside Numbers:

The place numbers, 4 and 10.

Over 7:

A bet that the next roll of the dice will produce a number greater than 7.

Parlay or Press:

The increase of a won bet, usually by doubling it.

Pass, Pass Line:

A bet made before a point is established, on the coming-out roll only, that the dice will pass, or win.

Pass Bet Decision:

A bet on pass that gets completed as either a winning or losing bet.

Payoff, House Payoff:

The amount of money the casino pays the player on a winning bet.

Place Bet:

A wager that a particular box number, whichever is bet on, the 4, 5, 6, 8, 9, or 10, will be rolled before a 7.

Point, Point Number:

The throw of a 4, 5, 6, 8, 9, or 10 on the coming-out roll becomes the point number.

Probability:

The ratio of the number of times that an event is likely to happen compared to the whole number of ways of which this particular event is a part. For example, the probability for having two dice add to 2 is 1 out of 36 rolls.

Proposition Bets:

See Center Bets.

Return:

The total amount returned to the bettor after he wins a bet including the sum of the amount he bet plus the amount he won. For example, if you bet $1 on a bet and win $2 more, your return would be $3. (Craps tables sometimes state payoffs with a for, as in "30 for 1," which means that a $1 bet will return $30 (not $31). Since $1 is the bet, the casino is actually paying 29 to 1, not the 30 to 1 they would like you to believe.)

Return Ratio:

The ratio of what the total return actually is compared to what it would have been had its true odds been applied to the win. For example, when $30 is returned for a winning bet on 2 when $36 would be the return at the true odds, the return ratio is 83.333% (30 ÷ 36 x 100).

Right Bettors:

Players betting that the dice will pass. Pass and come bettors.

Roll or Throw:

An individual toss of the dice.

Roller:

See Shooter.

Seven-Out:

The roll of a 7 after a point has been established, a loser for pass line bettors.

GLOSSARY

Shooter:

The player throwing the dice.

Single Odds:

A free-odds bet that allows the player to bet equal the pass or come bet as a right bettor, and equal the payoff on a don't pass or don't come bet.

Standoff:

A tie, nobody wins. Also called a Push.

Sucker Bets:

Exotic wagers (that is, bad wagers) with long odds that give the house an exorbitant edge against the player.

Trap Bet:

A bet that gives you the chance to increase the rate at which you can lose money.

Under 7:

A bet that the next roll of the dice will be a number that is less than 7.

Unit:

Bet size used as a standard of measurement.

Working:

Designation that a bet is "on," that is, in play.

Wrong Bettors:

Don't pass and don't come bettors.

THE CARDOZA CRAPS MASTER

Exclusive Offer! - Not Available Anywhere Else)

Three Big Strategies!

Here It is! **At last**, the **secrets** of the **Grande-Gold Power Sweep, Molliere's Monte Carlo Turnaround** and the **Montarde-D'Girard Double Reverse** - three big strategies - are made available and presented for the **first time anywhere**! These powerful strategies are designed for the serious craps player, one wishing to bring the best odds and strategies to hot tables, cold tables and choppy tables.

1. THE GRANDE-GOLD POWER SWEEP (HOT TABLE STRATEGY)

This **dynamic strategy** takes maximum advantage of hot tables and shows you how to amass small **fortunes quickly** when numbers are being thrown fast and furious. The Grande-Gold stresses aggressive betting on wagers the house has no edge on! This previously unreleased strategy will make you a powerhouse at a hot table.

2. MOLLIERE'S MONTE CARLO TURNAROUND (COLD TABLE STRATEGY)

For the player who likes betting against the dice, Molliere's Monte Carlo Turnaround shows how to turn a cold table into hot cash. Favored by an exclusive circle of professionals who will play nothing else, the uniqueness of this strongman strategy is that the vast majority of bets **give absolutely nothing away to the casino!**

3. MONTARDE-D'GIRARD DOUBLE REVERSE (CHOPPY TABLE STRATEGY)

This **new** strategy is the **latest development** and the **most exciting strategy** to be designed in recent years. **Learn how** to play the optimum strategies against the tables when the dice run hot and cold (a choppy table) with no apparent reason. **The Montarde-d'Girard Double Reverse** shows how you can **generate big profits** while less knowledgeable players are ground out by choppy dice. And, of course, the majority of our bets give nothing away to the casino!

BONUS!!!

Order now, and you'll receive **The Craps Master-Professional Money Management Formula** ($15 value) **absolutely free**! Necessary for serious players and **used by the pros**, the **Craps Master Formula** features the unique **stop-loss ladder.**

The Above Offer is Not Available Anywhere Else. You Must Order Here.

To order send ~~$75~~ $50 (plus postage and handling) by check or money order to:

Cardoza Publishing, P.O. Box 98115, Las Vegas, NV 89193